LAND, CAPITAL AND EXTRACTIVE FRONTIERS

Alternatives to Capitalism in the 21st Century

Series Editors: **Lara Monticelli**, *University College London* and **Torsten Geelan**, *University of Bristol*

Debates about the future of capitalism demonstrate the urgent need to envision and enact alternatives that can help tackle the multiple intertwined crises that societies are currently facing. This ground-breaking series advances the international, comparative and interdisciplinary study of capitalism and its alternatives in the 21st Century.

Also available in the series:

- *Creative Construction* edited by Jan Groos and Christoph Sorg
- *A Desire for Equality* by Michel Lallement
- *Remaking Money for a Sustainable Future* by Ester Barinaga Martín
- *Prefiguring Utopia* by Suryamayi Aswini Clarence-Smith
- *From Capital to Commons* by Hannes Gerhardt
- *Alternative Societies* by Luke Martell
- *Politics of the Gift* by Frank Adloff
- *The Future Is Now: An Introduction to Prefigurative Politics* edited by Lara Monticelli

Find out more at:

bristoluniversitypress.co.uk/alternatives-to-capitalism-in-the-21st-century

LAND, CAPITAL AND EXTRACTIVE FRONTIERS

Social Conflict and Ecological Crisis in the Senegal River Delta

Maura Benegiamo

With a Foreword by
Luigi Pellizzoni

Translated and updated by
Maura Benegiamo with support from
Daria E. Cavallini and Cordelia K. Bacci,
Centro Linguistico – Università di Pisa

Originally published in Italian by Orthotes in 2021 as
La terra dentro il capitale. Conflitti, crisi ecologica e sviluppo nel delta del Senegal

BRISTOL
UNIVERSITY
PRESS

First published in Great Britain in 2025 by

Bristol University Press
University of Bristol
1–9 Old Park Hill
Bristol
BS2 8BB
UK
t: +44 (0)117 374 6645
e: bup-info@bristol.ac.uk

Details of international sales and distribution partners are available at bristoluniversitypress.co.uk

British Library Cataloguing in Publication Data
A catalogue record for this book is available from the British Library

ISBN 978-1-5292-3782-5 hardcover
ISBN 978-1-5292-3783-2 ePub
ISBN 978-1-5292-3784-9 ePdf

Cover design: Liam Roberts
Front cover image: Land grabbing by Zualidro
Bristol University Press uses environmentally responsible print partners.
Printed and bound in Great Britain by CPI Group (UK) Ltd, Croydon, CR0 4YY

FSC
www.fsc.org
MIX
Paper | Supporting responsible forestry
FSC® C013604

To my mother, Maria Antonietta, and to the people living in the lands of the Ndiaël Avifauna Reserve and all the communities fighting for justice around the world

Contents

List of Figures

About the Author

Maura Benegiamo is Assistant Professor in Economic and Labour Sociology at the University of Pisa. She has conducted research and consultant activities across Europe, sub-Saharan Africa and Central America, focusing on environmental conflicts, natural resource extraction and agrarian development. Her research interests centre on the transformations of capitalism, labour and neoliberal governance within the context of the ecological crisis, with particular attention to extractivism, the role of techno-scientific innovation, political ecology and decolonial struggles. Her work has been published in various international scientific journals, and she is the creator of the documentary *Progreso7: Oro, armas y resistencia* (Guatemala-France, 2012), which documents resistance movements against large-scale mining in Guatemala.

Acknowledgements

Translating and updating this book is, for me, above all, an opportunity to amplify the echo of the stories and voices gathered here. I therefore thank those who, over the years, have enabled me to research and listen to them.

First and foremost, the Senegalese community, especially Salif Ka and Amadou Ka; Diatou Mbaye, the members of the collective for the defence of the lands of Ndiaël, Gourghi, Bayal, Aliu, Fatou, the women, men and children of Ndiaël, the villages of Kadun Deff and Djalbanabe. Thanks to Mariam Sow and Ardo Sow from Enda Pronat. My gratitude also extends to Luciana de Michele, Stefania and Stefano Lentati: this book owes much to you.

This book would not have been possible without an academic community that saw me grow and mature. First of all, I thank to Luigi Pellizzoni who have followed my research work from the beginning, Riccardo Ciavolella for the valuable exchanges during my visiting in Paris, and my colleagues from the VII cycle of the Iuav University of Venice doctoral programme. Thanks to Simone Arnaldi for encouraging and supporting me in publishing, and to Matteo Villa and the colleagues from the Department of Political Science at the University of Pisa, who welcomed my work, allowing me to focus on this translation.

A very special thanks goes to the POE (Politics-Ontology-Ecologies) research collective, and its members, from whom I have learned so much and who provided the fortune of a supportive academic space. I am also especially grateful to Emanuele Leonardi, Laura Centemeri, Viviana Asara, Alice dal Gobbo, Dario Minervini, Ivano Scotti, Gennaro Avallone, Roberto Saleri, Stefania Barca, Marco Armiero, and the entire Italian political ecology community. Thanks also to those who, over the years, have read, discussed and commented on my work, and to Diego Arturo Giordano for first hosting it within the Orthotes Political Ecology series.

Finally, in this fertile compost, my deepest thanks go to my family and friends for their constant support, presence and care, and to my son for all that he teaches me.

Foreword

Luigi Pellizzoni

With land capitalism has always played a double game. From land come the 'free gifts' on which accumulation depends; but precisely because they are free, for capital these goods are worth nothing in themselves. To acquire value they must be 'put to work', and to be 'put to work' they must be appropriated. As stated by Locke, who can be considered one of the founders of the ideology of capital, what originally belong to all can and should be privatized in order to motivate the owner to extract as much value as possible, for his (the male pronoun is mandatory!) and everyone's benefit.

From Marx to Weber, from Benjamin to Polanyi: many have argued that capitalism is more than an economy. To use a successful expression by Nancy Fraser, it is an institutionalized social order, in the same way that feudalism is. It thus includes not only an organization of economic relations but also a conception of reality, a morality and a structuring of the relations within and between all social spheres. By the same token, capitalism tends to hegemonize the sense of the world and the existence of those who dwell in it, crushing or denying the exterior, the other than oneself. Its peculiarity, however, lies, on one side, in that the crises it goes through are not accidental and disruptive events but structural and propulsive; on the other, on its extraordinary capacity to react to external threats. Capitalism has so far managed to incorporate, to mould in its own image, everything it has encountered on its way.

If any social order is never static, the question of 'continuity within change' or 'change within continuity' therefore arises most poignantly and dramatically for the capital order. What persists can be summed up in the validity, confirmed at each historical passage, of the Marxian formula M-C-M′. For capitalism, material reality is a mere pretext, a necessary step to achieve what really counts: the accumulation of capital. What changes, therefore, is what is most interesting and important, because it is precisely in this that we measure the challenge that takes place at the frontier of commodification, where capital encounters other worlds, human and more-than-human, with the specific resistances to assimilation that they develop.

The last few decades have marked a profound turning point in the history of capitalism. Post-Fordist globalization has been accompanied by the neoliberal 'revolution', at the heart of which, as Foucault has clearly grasped, lies a peculiar conception of social reality, seen as chaotic and therefore properly ungovernable, in the sense of not being amenable to pre-established order, complemented with an equally peculiar conception of the individual. Concealed in the latter's soul is seen to lie the *homo economicus*, the self-enterprising subject, committed to a continuous self-expansion, to bring out which targeted policies are required, first of all regulatory and educational. If, as has been said, any material economy implies a moral economy, a conception of what is right, dutiful and desirable, neoliberal capitalism has at its core an anthropology conceived at once as a starting point and a project to be realized, by hook or by crook. An author like Hayek is quite explicit about this.

The years of globalization and of the establishment of a neoliberal order are also years in which the very conception of biophysical reality has been profoundly challenged and modified. Undoubtedly, the game remains the same, as well described by Jason Moore and before him by Neil Smith. A game according to which land, with which humans, like any other living being, have an inseparable bond, has first to be rejected into a separate realm – that of 'nature', objectified and seen as passively reactive – and then included in production processes. Yet, globalization has resulted in the virtual exhaustion of planetary areas to be externalized, hence a risk for the game to end. The more capitalism spreads, therefore, the more it seems to be laying the grounds for its own downfall. It is the aporia denounced by Marx and extended by James O'Connor from labour to land, where it seems to take on a configuration that is difficult to get around (the 'limits to growth' denounced by the Club of Rome report in the early 1970s).

The response to this unprecedented challenge is twofold. On the one hand, the commodity frontier moves from the surface to the depths of the biophysical world. The 'internal grammar of nature' (to quote Nancy Fraser again) is increasingly altered in order to intensify the extraction of value. On the other hand, the narrative underlying this movement builds less and less on the epistemic level (geographical and scientific discoveries, extensions of property rights and so on), and increasingly on the ontological. The otherness of the non-social and the non-capitalist is ever more insistently presented as *already internal* to the social and to capital, of which it would constitute a mere variant or an as yet unexpressed form. The ecomodernist narrative of neoliberal think thanks and biotechnology industries says it loud and clear: nature is technology and technology is nature; just as the non-capitalist economy is a capitalist economy that is not (yet) able to recognize and valorize its own potential. There is no 'outside'; only internal differentiations within a single order of reality, where capital and the world are one and the same. This is also expressed by the Anthropocene narrative. The rapid rise of this notion from a stratigraphic hypothesis to a regulatory idea called upon to rewrite past, present and future can be explained only by its perfect coincidence with the spirit of the times; a coincidence that seems to capture even thinkers such as Dipesh Chakrabarty, who have built their careers on a postcolonial critique of the Western narrative. A further example is the impetuous growth of the economy of ecosystem services, now conceptually and concretely so far beyond the Polanyian 'fictitious commodities' as to affirm that the world is fully and originally a commodity, just waiting to be properly valued. In all evidence, this undermines the traditional conception and critique of capitalism, based on a neat distinction between production and reproduction. Such distinction is less and less discernible in current valorization processes. It is for this reason that ecofeminist thought, which for decades has been engaged in thematizing how the reproductive sphere is central to capital's order, is today in many ways the most advanced and vital tip of the critique.

The years of neoliberal globalization are also years in which the colonial legacy fully shows its weight, persistence and contradictions. The structural adjustment programmes with which an attempt was made to revive the unfulfilled promise of modernization have highlighted the 'necropolitical' (Achille Mbembe) character of the latter: the exclusion and marginalization that constitute its necessary complement in the form of unproductive waste, ways of life resistant to progress or irreducible to its demands, and therefore disposable. Coloniality has reasserted itself by assigning specific vocations to 'emerging' economies, to be opposed to the supposed immobility of traditional economies but, as found, bound to reinforce dependence on global economic circuits. The structuring of postcolonial states on the basis of the political and legal institutions of the West (or rather, versions of these institutions belonging to the former colonial powers of reference) then overlapped with the traditional divisions of local communities, giving rise to new inequalities and lacerations.

Compared to the this, the most recent years have marked a further change of pace. The turning point came with the 2007–2009 crisis, which simultaneously hit the financial and the food markets, in the context of ecological issues (climate change, loss of biodiversity, increasing difficulty of access to water and raw materials) that are taking on an increasingly concrete aspect; threats that are planetary but unpredictable and geographically uneven in their manifestations. Although apparently unconnected, the two crises are profoundly linked in that they both point to an increasingly dramatic disconnection between reality and the market, matter and money. For some, the crisis of capital realization, apart from contingent factors, can be traced back to a 'secular' trend towards stagnation. The latest technical revolutions (bio and ICT) have not produced a quantum leap in energy efficiency comparable to that of the industrial revolution. Their propulsive thrust is therefore already running out. In any case, monetary fluctuations show the hollowness of the neoliberal paradigm of 'food security', which has been imposed since the 1990s and is based on the idea that a neoliberal global market (competitive specialization) can provide everyone with access to food, wherever it is produced.

It is from these same years that the phenomenon of land-grabbing, of which Africa is a main scene, has taken shape. The contemporary 'race for land' is in line with an established model of industrial agriculture, that of the 'green revolution', based on monoculture, intensive exploitation and inclusion in global value chains, yet it shows some peculiarities. First, it expresses a renewed interest of the food industry in directly managing production sources. Second, the energy and the climate crises significantly orient land transactions towards non-food purposes, in particular biofuel production. Third, the fundamental function of land as a reserve available for all eventualities start to gain salience in this period, in the face of increasingly pronounced social, financial and ecological instabilities. It, however, differs from the rent-seeking drives characteristic of past moments of productive crisis, attesting rather the process of ontological acquisition of the world to the sphere of commodities that has already been mentioned and constitutes the most relevant, but also the most enigmatic (for traditional interpretations), cypher of contemporary capitalism. The importance of the reserve function, as generic opportunity, of land is also made evident by the fact that the 'land-grabbers' have sometimes no specific experience in the agrarian activities in which they are meant to engage.

It is precisely the issue of land-grabbing that Maura Benegiamo's book deals with – what it is, on what assumptions and motivations it is based, what role the colonial legacy plays in it, what it means for those who are affected by it, what forms of resistance it determines. The book offers an enlightening and engaging investigation into this phenomenon and more generally into today's capitalism: its peculiar traits; the exclusions and marginality it produces; its ecological impacts; the rejection of its logic that takes shape on the ridge of necropolitics. A rejection that, before being explicit opposition, expresses a profound incompatibility – what the author calls the 'physical impossibility of coexistence' – between capitalism and other ways of living, of relating to the biophysical world, of conceiving oneself, the human collectives and the bond between the human and the non-human.

The case on which the study focuses is emblematic. The story begins in 2010: an Italian company decides to acquire a 20,000-hectare plot of land in the Senegal River delta, with the aim of producing sunflowers and sweet potatoes for obtaining bioethanol. The story unfolds over a few years, intertwining with the political vicissitudes of the Senegal state, to end, at least provisionally, in 2017, with the withdrawal of the Italian investor following the basic failure of the project and also the growing hostility of the local communities. But the story the book tells is broader than that of a failed investment. What it shows is how land-grabbing continues the postcolonial developmental logic, in which international capital and local authorities are allied. The latter suffer it but also support it by any means, from the granting of exploitation permits of very long duration to the declassification of protected areas, to the acceptance of artfully constructed impact studies. The developmental logic, the book again shows, penetrates the fabric of local communities, dividing those who somehow have (or hope to have) something to gain and those who have everything to lose.

These latter, in the story analysed, are the long-time pastoral communities, characterized by a co-evolving relationship with a land of precarious hydro-geological equilibrium; a relationship based on a sense of place, time and space capable of maintaining this equilibrium in its constant change, thanks to an understanding of what is valuable that is completely foreign to the conception inherent to capitalist appropriation and industrial system. What from the point of view of development appears to be immobility, that is, inability to optimize the resources at one's disposal by accepting change and taking advantage of the opportunities they offer, is indeed a completely different vision of what remains and what changes. A vision whereby land is not something other than oneself, according to the categories of Western dualism, but something that proceeds together with the human collective.

Marginal among marginal (yet perfectly 'centred' with respect to the place they dwell), poor among the poor (yet not at all such, from their viewpoint), these communities are unsuitable even for the 'participatory' processes by which promoters and authorities seek to legitimize decisions already taken and to manage the discontent. They are irreducible to the category of 'stakeholder': what for them is important cannot be represented according to the logics overseeing the decision process. They can just be amenable to 'compensations': the 'philanthropy', the benevolence of capital, which everywhere is replacing rights more and more.

In the language spoken by these communities, the author reminds us, the word development does not exist; not in the capitalist sense, at least. Change is obviously there – it cannot be otherwise, nor can it remain unacknowledged in any socio-material assemblage – but not in the sense of a less and a more, a before and an after linearly connected. In the extensive and conservative logic of local pastoral practice there is a sense of optimization very different from value-extraction efficiency; more akin, if anything, to what in the West is called agro-ecology: the integration of the 'interests' of all, human and non-human, of yesterday, today and tomorrow, as they are inseparable from each other and therefore inconceivable in terms of opposition or overcoming. Thus, it is not surprising that the interviews reported in the book reveal that herders do not want to become agricultural wage workers, nor do they wish to adopt a business logic of intensive agro-pastoralism. It is not surprising as well that those who are accustomed to interacting with the land in a way so different from what the various versions of the Green Revolution propose display what the author describes as calm, composure, wisdom and dignity; a sense of place and collective by now almost entirely vanished in the West, vainly replaced by particularisms and invented traditions.

Maura Benegiamo's book recounts and reflects on all this, blending passion and reasoning with rare effectiveness and perspicacity. It is the narration of a personal experience, which one senses has been intense and profoundly formative, and a placing of this experience in the context of the overall dynamics of globalization. It is fastidious focalization on the details of a specific event, the peculiarities of a historical legacy, the uniqueness of places and cultures, interspersed with zooms backwards in the frame, to show the far-reaching, often unforeseen, trajectories that these peculiarities compose. One among many episodes of land-grabbing thus acquires significance against the backdrop of the twists and turns of global capitalism, while shedding valuable light on the latter. It is from books like this one – written by a brilliant and passionate scholar, belonging to a generation more disillusioned than mine but no less, indeed more, motivated to study the world, understand it and change it, putting to good use the wisdom that the world often holds where one does not expect to find it – that we can draw important pointers to reflect on the past, read the present, and imagine a future different from the one that the falsely inexorable logic of capital seems to impose.

Introduction: Colonial Fractures, Land-Grabbing and the Ecological Crisis of Capitalism

Colonial fractures and margins of resistance

Almost two hundred years ago, Baron Jacques-François Roger took up residence in his new home on the banks of the Senegal River, a majestic and eccentric neoclassical building that was much more princely than the one where he had lived in the nearby town of Saint Louis. He had arrived in Senegal a few years earlier to take possession of the palace that the King of France had commissioned, modelled on the luxury residences of colonial officials and plantation owners in Santo Domingo (Argo, 1976), at the time among the richest colonies of the French Empire. With the grand inauguration party that was held in the new residence, Roger probably wanted to give a specific character to his mandate. After several attempts, he had succeeded in obtaining the office of governor by royal stipulation on 26 July 1821 and was appointed *Commandant et administrateur du Sénégal et dépendances*. Mandated by the King of France to implement a policy of recovery and development of the colony, he carried out his project of building a model farm in the delta region of the Senegal River, before surrendering to failure. He left Senegal seven years later.

Determined to import the colonial plantation model to Senegal, Roger made a few attempts at developing irrigated agriculture and conducting cutting-edge botanical experiments in the delta. The species involved in his experiments were mainly rice, certain fruit trees, indigo, coffee and the peanut, the only plant that earned him considerable success and of which he became an ardent promoter. Roger was assisted in this project by the colony's French botanist and head gardener, Jean Michel Claude Richard, after whom the botanical park was later named. The park was built by Baron Roger in the vicinity of his palace, which now also gives its name to the small town of Richard Toll, from a Wolof word meaning 'garden'. That was the beginning of a long scientific career for Richard, which would lead him to travel to many islands and French colonies in Africa. However, he failed to go down in history as the great inventor he would have wished to be known as. In 1840 Elmond Albius – a 12-year-old slave who lived on the Island of Bourbon (currently named Réunion) – discovered what is still today the main technique for pollinating the vanilla flower, but Richard tried to claim paternity for it, asserting that he was the inventor. He was proved wrong, and his reputation was tarnished forever while Réunion Island would long retain its primacy as the main exporter of vanilla, including the prized Bourbon variety.

It took another 120 years to dismantle the colonial system in Senegal. Roger's palace now lies in ruins in the delta, but his project has not died out. Today, the region is the main centre of rice production in the country, its watercourses have all been gradually channelled to irrigate the farmers' fields and allow agriculture to advance on what was previously a vast area almost entirely covered by swamps, ponds and wetlands. From December to June, if you follow the road from Richard Toll to the town of Ross Bethio, 50 kilometres further south, and look to the right, you will see some of these irrigated fields. To the left are the semi-desert expanses of the Sahelian dry season, dotted with only a few small groups of huts. You need to leave the road and enter the savannah to discover a new, different vegetation, interspersed with numerous acacia and baobab trees and the presence of a few herds of cows, sheep, goats and donkeys. This is where, at least until 2012, the Ndiaël Avifauna Reserve was located.

When I reached the area in 2013, I had just arrived in Senegal with the intention of closely investigating one of the large land acquisitions that had affected the continent in the aftermath of the 2007–2008 world food price crisis and in the years immediately following. At that time, the news that, globally, land had been changing hands at a pace and concentration unseen since colonial times had begun to circulate even in the non-specialist media. As suggested by the timing of these operations, in most cases it was an attempt to respond and adapt to the major climatic, ecological, food, energy and financial crises that the planet was going through. Many of those operations were also driven by a series of new agricultural development and energy transition policies sanctioned globally and by individual states. It was, however, a phenomenon of staggering proportions. According to official estimates of that period, at least 45 million hectares of arable land had changed hands in 2008–2009 alone (Deininger and Byerlee, 2011); higher estimates emerged in the period immediately following the investment peak (Edelman et al, 2013). Most of the acquisitions involved areas between 10,000 and 200,000 hectares. With more than half of recorded transactions, the African continent – and sub-Saharan Africa in particular – was among the areas most affected by this process. Entire chunks of territory were passing through the hands of opaque financial groups and actors on the basis of hazy processes (Anseeuw et al, 2012).

I knew that I would most likely be faced with a conflict between capitalist companies and local communities whose members did not want to be dispossessed of their lands. I did not imagine, however, that the history I would document would also have to do with the rhythm of river floods and ocean tides or with the succession of rains and long periods of drought that played a central role in the evolution of the region, well before French colonization. This also meant studying the morphology of the soils and their spatial distribution, the position of the clay depressions, and knowing where the sand dunes ended or the barren, lateritic expanses began. Little did I know that I would end up reconstructing the genesis of that conflict and of those places from far back in time, looking for traces in the historical archives of the Société nationale d'aménagement et d'exploitation des terres du delta du fleuve Sénégal, in the theses of agronomy students at Dakar and Saint Louis universities, and in the reports of former French colonial institutes. Yet, the history of a territory that had existed but was no longer there proved to be the main key to analysing what was happening in those areas. Secondly, it was necessary to look at capitalist development not so much, or not only, as the process underlying the evolution of the market and private property, but also as the continuous alteration of living spaces and the reorganization of the rhythms of regeneration and forms of reproduction of species, including the human one.

A few scholars, including anthropologist Anna Tsing, have proposed to define our era as the age of plantations. This approach embraces the results of the analyses of many historians, geographers and scholars of world history and the Anthropocene (Haraway et al, 2016), and proposes to trace the emergence of a particular conjunction between the 'discipline of plants' (Haraway and Tsing, 2019) and that of labour back to the colonial project. This conjunction would eventually inform the entire social structures of modernity in the process that saw plantation economy expand in the islands of the Caribbean Sea, from Barbados to Jamaica, in the early 15th century. The logic of plantations revolved around the labour of thousands of African slaves and caused the extinction of entire peoples and cultures, plants, microbes and animals. Not only did it impose a radical simplification of the forms of life on those lush islands, but it also influenced the forms of spatial planning and required the creation of regulatory norms and standards that are still in use today.

Plantations have changed the geography of places and of circulation on a global scale, creating new infrastructures and technologies and allowing urban centres to expand. As explained by Jason Moore (2015), this massive project to rewrite the 'world-systems' was primarily aimed at creating a 'cheap' nature that made resources and food available to the expanding proletariat in the emerging industrial economies of Europe at low prices. Of course, this did not happen immediately; many other processes were to unfold to make it a reality. For instance, most women were assigned to activities that were deemed worthless, unproductive and for which there was no pay, such as looking after children, preparing food, caring for the sick, collecting herbs and firewood in the forest. In order to 'free the men' and turn them into wage labourers, vast tracts of land had to be privatized. Finally, without the intense and increasing exploitation of fossil minerals, neither agriculture nor industry could have evolved the way they did.

Over the last two decades, the problem of ensuring an accessible and sufficient food supply to a growing global urban population has regained a central place in scientific and development policy debates. Several factors have contributed to this renewed centrality of the food issue, first and foremost the exacerbation, between 2007 and 2008, of a global food price crisis that caused the number of people suffering from hunger or undernourishment to exceed one billion for the first time since 1970 (FAO, 2009a).[1] The debate on agriculture was also influenced by the presence of a global rural and peasant movement, which has been gaining strength since the early 1990s, highlighting the central role that can be played by small famers in ensuring fair, inclusive and sustainable societies and in radically changing the ways food is produced, distributed and consumed.

Albeit from very different and substantially divergent perspectives, both the food crisis and the rural movements are part of a crisis that involves 'cheap food' as well as the world and geopolitical system within which such food is produced. More than anything else, the 'cheap food' model in the rural areas of the so-called 'global South'[2] has caused hunger and environmental disasters. In fact, from the 1980s onwards, many people have been forced to migrate to the slums of fast-expanding megalopolises (Davis, 2006), selling or losing their land, as it was swallowed up into monoculture systems, the building of large infrastructure works or the new mining projects that multiplied throughout the 1990s and 2000s. Nevertheless, small-scale and peasant agriculture has continued, albeit with difficulties, to be the main provider of food, particularly in the lowest income countries, guaranteeing thousands of people the right to nutrition. This is explained by the fact that these activities are mainly oriented towards food production and favour the national context in order to sell their surpluses in regional and local markets. They follow a production and market logic that is distinct from those applied by the agro-industrial sector controlled by large corporations, which tends to favour non-food use of the agricultural produce, mainly for exports and subject to the variations in financial markets.

In the aftermath of the 2007–2008 food crisis, the framework outlined earlier has undergone deep changes that are radically reshaping the material conditions and power relations in many contexts. These processes threaten to definitively undermine the capacity of small-scale household farmers to guarantee their self-sufficiency and supply local markets, bringing more and more people into that margin of exclusion constituted by lives whose reproduction now seems to be unnecessary for the development of capitalism (Li, 2017).

Both the food crisis and the ways in which it was being responded to are still within the system that generated them. Capitalism is accustomed to crises and dealing with them is part of its way of advancing. As David Harvey (2007a) explains, one central mechanism of response is the geographical circulation and expansion of capital and, at the same time, its landing in specific places, which undergo deep restructuring before eventually being abandoned. A second mechanism, peculiar to neoliberal capitalism, is that of appropriating the common wealth in order to increase one's own power and profit from new commodities. In this framework, fundamental mechanisms are the commodification and privatization of land and the conversion of various forms of goods – common, collective, state, and so on – into exclusive private property rights (Harvey, 2007b). Capitalism cyclically needs to extract value from the practices underlying what Marx called primitive or original accumulation.

While much of that thinking remains valid, what was happening in the context of the new land rush also highlighted other dynamics. In fact, it seemed that issues such as the value of nature, water, biodiversity, and the possibility of securing a supply of basic goods, played a primary role not so much, or not only, as strategies of value production and accumulation, but as guarantees of the reproduction of the capitalist system itself and at the same time an attempt to incorporate and bend the forms of reproduction into new circuits of value and trade. The global reconfiguration of capitalism in the face of ecological contradiction, summarized in the cheap food crisis (see also Patel and Moore, 2017), therefore takes the form of a further expansion of extractive frontiers and an even more profound and irreversible modification of ecosystems, life and reproduction on Earth. When observed at a local level, these dynamics allow us to look at the great social transformations with a decolonized gaze. They show themselves as crises, metamorphoses and resistances that are materially embedded in the relationships, territories and forms of subjectivity.

One evening in March several years ago, when the sun had already set over the village of D. in the Ndiaël Reserve, I was struck by lights silhouetted on the horizon, very different from those of the camp fires that illuminate the night in this part of the Sahelian savannah. The people with me explained that they were the headlights of the tractors preparing the land for sowing, uprooting the shrubs that were growing wild and that, until then, had fed the animals. It was not clear how long they would take, whether weeks or months, but it was known that they intended to proceed until they reached the village gates. Soon after, while sitting on the ground with a few elders and some very young boys who had returned to Senegal after an attempt to migrate to Spain, I listened to reflections that seemed new for that context. The adults wondered whether they might have been wrong in keeping young people out of political claims and negotiations, and whether it might be necessary to adopt new breeding methods as well as to resort to new strategies in order to achieve broader forms of representation within the dominant power structures. A. Sow, however, seemed distracted. He later told me that he was thinking back to when, long ago, his family had come here to build the first settlements, travelling north-west up the routes that brought the herders from the red lands of the Cajor desert to the shores of Lake Guiers to water their animals and in search of unoccupied pastures. If he were to leave – he thought – he would not be as lucky, because all the water was for those who cultivated the fields, and the government seemed to prefer to assign land to the new entrepreneurs coming to Senegal with means and capital. He also thought that perhaps the time had come for change, but he could not associate this word to a valid or feasible scenario.

Sometime later, during a group discussion organized with some villagers in Ndiaël, a woman who was sitting a little further away from the first circle of people stood up and took the floor. She exclaimed: 'What worries us as livestock farmers is not so much our fate, but above all that of our children and grandchildren: the Fulɓe people live off pastoralism and, if the project continues, livestock farming will disappear from this region, and this worries us deeply.'[3] I was struck not only by her words, but especially by the anxiety they conveyed. In her book *Land's End: Capitalist Relations on an Indigenous Frontier?* anthropologist Tania Li (2014a) proposes a slightly different interpretation of the idea of dispossession, reflecting on the fact that land-grabbing processes are often very long and take place across generations. Extractive frontiers, whether agricultural or mining, sometimes advance slowly, and occupy spaces progressively. These processes are not always immediately perceived as problems; sometimes the inhabitants of a given area can also get advantages, for instance, a new road being built or trades being established. The land in these places, writes Li, is often considered abundant, and the idea that there may no longer be enough space for all forms of life to evolve and adapt mutually is not immediately clear to its inhabitants. At a certain point, however, the land runs out and the people who initially managed to avoid or minimize their relationship with the frontier find themselves squeezed to a limit that is both spatial and social, and they become marginalized. The struggles and claims that arise in these contexts are often treated as struggles to defend the status quo and addressed by the institutions with the language of development and modernization and the imperative to adapt.

This, however, tends to overshadow the fact that, precisely because of the history from which they stemmed, these struggles sustain transformational dynamics that look to the future and move, along with many others, within an ambitious and multifaceted political space whose aim is attempting to find a balance between social well-being and continuity of life, regeneration and work, autonomy and participation, breakaway from colonial history and the possibility for other histories to emerge in the present. In this context, the analysis of 'socio-environmental conflicts' therefore develops along two distinct lines. On the one hand, the intention to bring out different ways of describing and understanding capitalist development, to highlight the processes through which several practices have been incorporated and marginalized in the economic and political structures of modernity. On the other hand, the need to focus on how, today, these same practices also create spaces from which it is possible to start again and imagine the transition to more just and sustainable forms of cohabitation.

Understanding land-grabbing: extractivism, crises and green capitalism

The debate on the socio-ecological crisis, its origins, implications and possible ways out is far from over: we need multifaceted analyses capable of connecting the different temporalities, subjectivities and ways of living through the crisis; of investigating the tensions and conflicts at play, as well as the alternative experiences already underway. Yet, to do so, as the notion of Capitalocene, Plantationocene and other similar notions attest (San Román and Molinero-Gerbeau, 2023), it is critical to shift our attention to the analysis of the socio-environmental relationships established in capitalist modernity to recognize how the destruction of nature and social oppression have historically been interconnected, and must be addressed together. It is therefore not enough to emphasize the failure of the current green neoliberal strategies in (not) addressing the climate crisis, but it is also crucial to dismantle the 'master narratives' (Barca, 2020) and rationales that still support the establishment of capitalism as an 'institutional social order' (Fraser, 2014) globally. One, as the postcolonial and ecofeminist critique largely demonstrated (Plumwood, 2002 [1993]; Salleh, 2017), in which the relations between human and non-human natures are (re)produced in and through systems of domination.

In this sense, the need to re-examine the long history of accumulation regimes in order to identify the roots of the climate crisis is not just about historical analysis, but also about the effects on the contemporary sociological and political debate on the definition of capitalism and the forms of power that sustain it. It is also in line with the claims emerging from many racialized, Black, women's and indigenous communities struggling for environmental and climate justice worldwide (Bullard, 2001). By denouncing the historical forms of oppression functional to capitalist valorization, these movements have often combined anti-capitalist demands with the request for a safe life in a safe environment (Vergés, 2021; Ferdinand, 2022).

Embedded within these perspectives, this book situates itself within the debate on decolonial political ecologies on one hand, and discusses the emerging relationship between global land-grabbing, extractivism and green capitalism on the other, thus also aspiring to contribute to a discussion on the transformation of capitalism in the context of the ecological crisis (Moore and Liley, 2011; Taşdemir Yaşın, 2017; Leonardi and Benegiamo, 2021). More precisely, it aims to contribute to a critique of capitalist political ecology through the analysis of global responses to the crisis of reproduction in and of today's capitalism, which are, among other things, pushing for extractivist logic on land and nature exploitation.[4] It compares these dynamics with local perspectives, which have been shaped by the experience of capitalist colonial modernity and are now grappling with green and neoliberal approaches to development. In this sense, following Enrique Leff's statement, this book also aligns with the idea of political ecology as 'the field in which power strategies for the social appropriation of nature are manifested and deployed: for the distribution of ecological costs and potentials in the construction of sustainability' (Leff, 2022, p 4, own translation).

In line with these objectives, this book articulates the analysis of a local case study with the analysis of a global phenomenon, that of the land rush of the early 2000s and the consequent reconfiguration of global policies on food security and their overlap with energy transition strategies particularly in Senegal, Europe and Italy. The research work was structured around the study of a socio-environmental conflict that arose following a large-scale agricultural project led by Italian investors whose aim was to grow sweet potatoes and sunflowers for import to Italy to produce green energy.[5] To account for local dynamics and impacts, the study combines elements of environmental history in the Senegal River delta and the analysis of colonial and postcolonial development policies with the study of the investment's governance mechanisms and local responses. It incorporates these elements with an ethnographic perspective interrogating the reality of pastoral communities opposed to land cession, giving visibility to an alternative way of living, and responding to the current socio-ecological crisis. The connection between global and local, and the continuous cross-references between the two scales, structures the book's narration aiming at fuelling a multi-level political ecology analysis of land use and access in the context of capitalist responses to the ecological crisis, showing the implications of these processes from different perspectives.

Since 2017, the Senhuile-Senethanol agro-industrial project – this being the name of the joint venture led by the Italian investors to acquire the necessary land in Senegal – has been discontinued. Due to poor performance in terms of agricultural yield and the growing hostility of the populations living on the land allocated by the government to the company, the Italian investors decided to leave the area. The shares were sold to a Senegalese partner that seems to have taken over the concession through a new company. Neither the individual investment nor its failure coincides with the end of the land-grabbing process, which remains an open possibility, both for the government, which plans to reallocate land to new entrepreneurs, and for the local populations, whose right to reside in the territory is called into question and made ever more uncertain by the current circumstances. Likewise, the vision of global land-grabbing as a unitary event and as the main indicator of the transformation of agro-industrial capitalism needs to be questioned. First of all, contrary to the reductionist perception of land-grabbing as a homogeneous phenomenon, several studies have pointed out that the land deals that have taken place since the 2007–2008 crisis involve a complex and multi-fold set of both local and global economic actors, interests and dynamics. Similarly, the reactions of the populations involved, as well as the forms of protest or collaboration, vary enormously. The land rush phenomenon itself has undergone major 'adjustments'. The main one, which is also analysed in this volume, is the waning interest in certain types of production, such as those related to Jatropha, and in certain lands – the most arid or marginal ones – which have been more difficult to exploit because they are far from transport networks or freshwater reserves.

This was not about dismissing the debate on new land acquisitions, but rather gaining a more detailed perception of the ways in which land is redefining itself as a central resource for the development of capitalism. Other scholars, however, have observed how the emphasis on large-scale land acquisitions risks overshadowing the multiple forms of land centralization occurring in the agro-industrial sector (foremost among which is the rise of contract farming initiatives), but also the forms of value extraction associated with land and the way in which territories are turned to profit (Oliveira et al, 2021). Initially, at a time when land transactions were multiplying, the expression 'land-grabbing' was useful to identify and define an ongoing trend, outlining its main characteristics. However, it soon became important to deepen the analysis in order to understand the phenomenon in light of the global changes and of the transformation dynamics underway at a local level.

It is in light of these concerns that the notion of extractivism proves particularly pertinent in accounting for a structural tendency in contemporary development dynamics associated with land exploitation and with different processes of resource grabbing. It is also particularly relevant in the analysis of the socio-material relations that nurture the current processes of green capitalism. The latter can be empirically defined as a model of climate governance based on the dual assumption that economic growth is not 'simply' compatible with environmental mitigation, but also that responses to the climate crisis can be a vector for the expansion of capitalism and the market system (Tienhaara, 2013; Leonardi, 2019). This reinforced the belief that free-market mechanisms, including private property and entrepreneurial freedom, are the best way to mitigate anthropogenic climate change, while promoting new processes of the commodification of nature. It therefore represents an ideological construction that crucially, and at the same time, innovatively restructures capitalist development, as it bases its legitimacy on a hypothesis that is also a gamble, that is, the total indifference between capitalism and the natural world (Pellizzoni, 2015; Battistoni, 2017). Promoting a further commodification of nature based on a market-oriented understanding of socio- ecological dynamics.

Green capitalism currently represents a major attempt at reorganizing the relationship between capitalism and nature in the search for a new socio-ecological capitalist regime (Cooper, 2008). However, as depicted by the land-grabbing phenomenon, which in fact had as its main driver the race for agrofuels, the gamble of a green capitalist regime does not foresee social inclusion as an effective prospect. This is in line with neoliberal perspectives but also with the persistence of colonial forms of power centred on valorization/devaluation processes. The question, however, is to better grasp the connections between this logic and that of an agro-industrial expansion increasingly driven by the principle that land is *needed*, but *labour is not* (Li, 2011).

This is particularly evident in the 'extractive commodities frontier contexts', where the inclusion of resources takes place within a general reorganization of pre-existing socio-ecological relations (Kröger, 2021). In a similar vein, Saskia Sassen points out that global land-grabbing processes follow an economic logic where rural spaces are regarded as central resources, not the people who live in them: 'the center of this logic is not the "valuing" of people as workers and consumers, but the expulsion of people and the destruction of traditional capitalisms to feed the needs of high finance and the needs for natural resources' (Sassen, 2010, p 25). But what exactly does this mean, from a capitalist point of view, that people are no longer valued as workers, to the point that they seem to have become redundant to capital accumulation? What exactly is new in this process and how is this related to the exploitation of nature?

The notion of extractivism provides useful insights to answer these questions and connect them with different dynamics of exploitation and expropriation that underpin accumulation processes. At the centre of an expanding debate (Ye et al, 2020; Chagnon et al, 2022), the concept designates a model of accumulation that extracts value from the provision of resources for global markets, while devaluing labour and ecologies at the local scale. Rooted in a strong colonial world ecology legacy, the establishment of an extractivist oriented economy has been firmly promoted under the neoliberal expansion of global commodity frontiers (Moore, 2000)[6] associated with a phase of capitalist orientation towards an even greater accumulation by dispossession (Harvey, 2007a). In this context, similar to the notion of land-grabbing, the idea of extractivism has played an important role in allowing various conflicts and resistances to recognize themselves within a common path, defined by the struggle against similar logic, albeit with differences in terms of implementation.

Analytically, the concept was first theorized at the end of the 1990s and 2000s in the context of the Latin American academic debate committed to updating theories of dependency and accounting for a new phase of economic policy on the continent, marked by the expansion of mega-mining projects and intensive monocultures (Svampa, 2019). According to Eduardo Gudynas (2009; 2015), for instance, extractivism represents a 'specific regime of accumulation' and is a 'style of development based on the appropriation of Nature'. It implies 'the appropriation of natural resources in large volumes and/or high intensity, where half or more are exported as raw materials, without industrial processing or with limited processing' (Gudynas, 2018, p 62). It delineates a model of territorial occupation that has often been seen through the political lens of the 'state of exception' (Zibechi, 2020).

In recent years however, the category of extractivism has expanded to embrace other resource exploitation dynamics and logic, including data and financial extractivism. Resorting to this concept has been particularly relevant in the debate about the logic and impact of 'green' environmental policies, with regard to, for example, the extraction of rare minerals needed for the energy transition; the construction of mega wind farms or photovoltaic parks; the conversion of forests and rural areas into providers of carbon credits and ecosystem services; and the production of agrofuels. New specifications, such as that of green extractivism or agrarian extractivism, have emerged, depending also on the type of dynamic on which the emphasis was to be placed: the new forms of valorization of nature, and the transformation of agro-industrial logic related to this.

The notion of green extractivism resonates with the idea of green-grabbing, namely the foreign appropriation of land and resources for environmental reasons (Fairhead et al, 2012), and focuses on new processes of the capitalization of nature in the name of the environment often driving dynamics of accumulation by dispossession and resource enclosure (Bruna, 2023). The idea of agro-extractivism, instead, has become established in the critical agrarian debate in reference to a specific form of agrarian accumulation based on predatory, rather than labour-inclusive, logic, and on the intensive-extensive exploitation of natural resources, with ruinous and irreversible social and environmental consequences (McKay et al, 2021). This differs from the more classic agro-industrial exploitation schemes precisely because of the 'underdevelopment' of productive forces and the fact that it resorts to monopolistic logic, extractive technologies, economies of scale and financialization to realize profit (Akram-Lodhi, 2021). This concept in particular emerged in relation to the expansion of agrofuel and flex-crop cultivation, which primarily affected Central American territories (Alonso-Fradejas, 2015).

These observations generate further questions such as what are the socio-ecological implications of an extractivist development process? What forms of governance does this imply? What justifications do these processes bring into play, what ideas and narratives do they draw on? What are the political responses that arise? In an attempt to provide a definition that brings together a diverse body of literature, Ye et al (2020), for example, define extractivism as a process in which production is based on the destruction of landscapes and biodiversity, making their reproduction materially impossible. They also emphasize how extractivism is based on 'available resources' that it does not contribute to creating or reproducing. However, making a resource available is a strictly political process, as it is imposing market value as the main form of valuation of a natural resource, structuring socio-ecological relations accordingly.

Beyond the large-scale and intensive exploitation model, extractivism also establishes specific relationships with the components of socio-ecological reproduction, including non-commodified labour and sustainability. These relationships create distinct logics of resource valorization, which combine with historically determined power relations to shape value accumulation in the postcolonial context. Extractivism does not occur in a vacuum, but articulates with pre-existing systems of exploitation and exclusion and requires political mediation at a local level. Here, moreover, it often encounters forms of resistance already in place, as well as specific problems and criticalities related to local ecologies and policies. This encounter, from which the research animating this book stems, opens the space for a rethinking of today's capitalist political ecology, in order to decolonize the perception of the ecological crisis and responses to it, in the shaping of a more just, reparative and ecological future. Yet however, it also stresses how current development patterns are directly involved in producing a residual population, which also means that marginality is not an accidental outcome that will be overcome with more development.

Book structure

As touched on earlier, by tracing the 'long history' of current land appropriations and highlighting the colonial character inherent in the formation processes of extractive frontiers, as in the Senhuile-Senethanol case, this book grasps the complexity of land-grabbing within a certain idea of capitalism. In order to be understood, this idea requires a different explanation of the logic of capitalist development, dwelling on the combination between new processes of valorization and the form of territorial exploitation, between production and reproduction, paying attention to the resistance generated in the various communities affected how this influences development trajectories.[7] In line with this objective, Chapter 1 deals with the territories involved with the

Italian investors in order to look at the ways in which landscapes, practices and communities have been reorganized and restructured in the context of specific social and ecological relations connected to ideas of development and modernization as defined by colonial planning and, subsequently, by the nation-state. Land enclosure through agricultural delimitation and the exclusion of herders from one of its places of excellence are accompanied by a development perspective that interprets land as an empty space; a space that can be occupied and domesticated according to precise hierarchies of knowledge, which continue to operate in the context of current investments. It is in this context that new extractivist dynamics articulate themselves with the colonial heritage over territories and landscapes, superimposing a global socio-ecological crisis on the already existing local socio-ecological crisis.

As stated, the analysis of the ongoing 'primitive accumulation', that is, the study of the relations between accumulation, dispossession and exclusion, must also be related to the evolution of global capitalism and the extended reproduction of agro-industrial capital, within the framework of ongoing systemic changes. For this reason, Chapter 2 moves towards a global level, that of the commodity price crisis that exploded in 2007–2008, closely followed by the financial crisis, from which *land-grabbing* emerged as a project and a concrete possibility for development. These mutually interconnected crises were more than a capitalist crisis in the classical sense of the term. The renewed centrality of the food question and the realignment of a large part of global development strategies around the question of agrarian productivity and agro-energy production have been the inkling that the framework within which the crisis of cheap food has unfolded should be traced back not only to capital valorization, labour exploitation and market exchange, but also to the more general limits of the social and ecological reproduction of the global capitalist system.

In this context, the responses by governments and agro-industrial, financial or entrepreneurial actors in search of new business perspectives have been to secure a resource – land – not only to realize value from it, but also with a view to a future of growing scarcity and ever more frequent emergencies. The deep sense of this move becomes clear when analysed within the general discourse on green capitalism development, according to which economic growth, food security and climate mitigation are not only compatible but can even reinforce each other. It is within this perspective that a new phase of food security policies is taking hold, led by the alliance of the technoscientific sector with major industrial and financial capitals.

Yet, it is not enough to associate the issue of the climate crisis to that of food security perspectives. These might suggest that sustainability can be achieved by renewing – and intensifying – production models, but – as already noted – the ecological question requires us to rethink the modern, colonial paradigm of infinite growth, rather than deal with its effects. Failure to recognize this is tantamount to concealing the fact that experimenting on the limits, and attempting to expand the frontiers of value, creates an ever-increasing margin of exclusion. The case of the delta shows this in a twofold way: on the one hand, it is no longer the peasants, the local farmers, who are at the centre of the new development strategies, but rather big agrarian capital supported by the government. On the other hand, for those who had already been condemned as incompatible with the modernist and developmentalist logic, there no longer seems to be any room for coexistence. In showing this, Chapter 3 goes into how some of the main narratives have guided the new food security policies: that of developmentalist modernization, that of agrofuels as a development driver for poor areas, and that of private investors as actors capable of combining economic growth, energy transition and improvement of local life. It explores these narratives by focusing on Senegal's development policies in the postcolonial period, on one hand, and the contradictions of Italy's agrofuels strategy, on the other. It further describes how these two 'political trajectories' interact in the current Senegalese strategy to attract foreign land investment shaping its main impacts and failure. The case of Italy is particularly emblematic in this context. Italian companies acquired extensive land in Senegal with the aim of producing agrofuels, but almost all of their projects failed within a few years.

This brings out a paradoxical dynamic at the heart of capitalist development. On the one hand, it highlights the continuous failures of development perspectives to achieve the promise of well-being and inclusion, the reasons for which are closely linked to the specific vision underlying the three narratives analysed. On the other, it also shows the hegemonic force of these same visions, which contributes to their success as they end up creating, through the material destruction of alternatives, the reality initially postulated. Capitalism, through the system of private property and the subjugation of reproductive needs to the creation of value, generates multiple dynamics of scarcity (instead of widespread abundance) in the name of which the logic of the market, competition and private interest, as a way of obtaining goods in the self-regulated market, becomes sensible.

By focusing on developmental narratives in these terms, this chapter implicitly draws on the notion of common sense in Gramsci, also echoing its use in the analyses of neoliberalism proposed by David Harvey (2007a, pp 39–40). Common sense, which differs from the idea of good sense (which stems instead from a critical perspective), encompasses the set of beliefs, visions and ideologies that structure hegemonic thinking about the world, thus sustaining a power bloc. Yet, as the postcolonial debate has greatly contributed to clarifying, common sense is also entangled and sustained by Western concepts of universality and subjecthood (Fanon, 2005), requiring at the same time a critique and a decolonization of knowledge (Leff, 2002 [1998]). The description of how Senhuile carried out its operations in the area is particularly fitting for this reasoning, proving that the failure of the development project also depends on the reiteration – implied in those narratives – of an almost ontological lack of understanding of the other's needs and other territorialities.

To account for this 'otherness', Chapter 4 offers a different point of view and attempts to grasp from an emic perspective the 'moral economy' specific to the Fulani rural world, the implications of the Senhuile-Senethanol investment and the forms of resistance it encounters. It also adopts an approach centred on narratives as units of analysis, giving space to what has been defined as narratives of environmental justice (Houston, 2013) according to which subjects who often suffer from different forms of environmental injustice present their experiences and define the issues at the core of the conflict in different ways (Armiero et al, 2019). It is the ethnographic method that serves as the main tool of investigation, combined with an analysis of the distortions of the governance processes involved in managing the territorialization of investment.

Special attention will be paid to corporate social responsibility procedures, and how they convey new rules and mode of governing, which in turn pave the way for the redefinition of social relations related to land and resources. Against this backdrop, ethnographic enquiry and participatory observation were aimed at analysing the meanings that people gave to the events involving them. This also makes it possible to place them within a horizon of meaning, and to investigate the ways in which they confront and relate to power, constructing political translations of social problems. The interviews conducted thus allow us to focus on, and question, the hierarchy of the forms of life and their ontological negation at the heart of capitalist development. At the same time, they give visibility to alternative ways to conceive development, labour and solutions to crises.

Finally, the Conclusion summarizes the key insights and findings of the book, linking them to the latest developments in the studied cases and analysed policies. Additionally, it reflects on the transformative potential of contemporary socio-ecological struggles in postcolonial contexts to respond to the crisis in more just and sustainable ways and on possible transnational alliances.

Figure 0.1: Senegal River delta

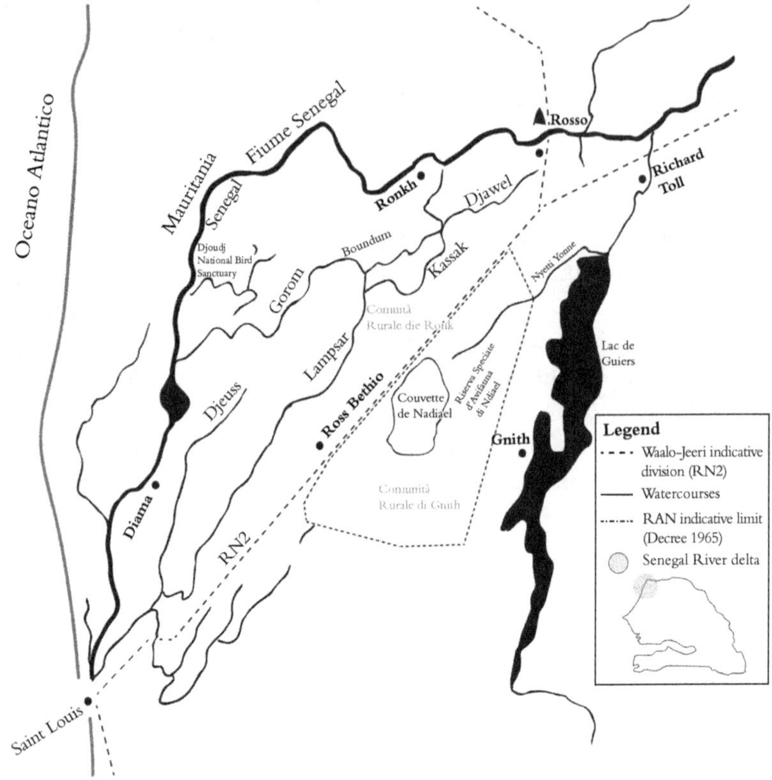

Note: Representation of the delta region, on the Senegalese side, its watercourses and the Waalo-Jeeri separation.

Source: Author

1

New Frontiers, Old Margins

Growing sunflowers in the Ndiaël Avifauna Reserve

Towards the end of the summer of 2010, an Italian company producing edible oil and active in the agro-energy market decided to partner with an entrepreneur of long-standing experience in the agro-industry to make an investment in Senegal. The project involved the acquisition of an expanse of land on which to cultivate sunflower and sweet potato for the subsequent production of bioethanol. However, over the following years, the purpose behind the crops being cultivated changed many times and at one point included the cultivation of rice for food purposes, but returns were always very poor if not irrelevant. What has remained a constant over the years is the amount of land considered necessary for the investment: 20,000 hectares, that is, an area roughly the size of Milan and two and a half times the city of Dakar, equivalent to 28,000 football pitches.[1]

In Senegal, as in many other African states, the land tenure regime is a mix of formal and informal systems. Here, moreover, private property is less widespread than national land property, a juridical category that gives land an inalienable and collective character.[2] All rural areas fall under this group and so they cannot be the object of individual property but only of use rights. Therefore, to obtain the right to access such land, the joint venture had to seek permission from the rural community, which represents the first level of administrative power and presides over land concessions.[3]

The negotiations were conducted by two Senegalese companies, specially created for the occasion, which worked together to obtain the concession. The first, called Senethanol, had a wealthy Senegalese businessman and a shell company set up in New York years before for the purpose of 'any lawful business' as its main shareholders; the second, Senhuile, was the Senegalese subsidiary of the Italian company.[4] The area initially targeted for the investment was in the rural community of Fanaye, located roughly halfway up the Senegal River Valley. Although the company managed to obtain consent from the president of the Fanaye Rural Community and was granted the 20,000 hectares, the investment was soon to be stopped by the then Senegalese President Abdoulaye Wade in response to violent local protests that resulted in the death of two people. However, this did not mean the end of the project, also because Wade himself almost immediately delocalized the concession in the Senegal River delta region, in the extreme west of the Vallée, on the lands of the Ndiaël Avifauna Reserve. Without the need to intercede with the rural community, this time the 20,000 hectares were allocated through a double presidential decree that declassified part of the reserve and granted a concession on the area to the Senhuile-Senethanol consortium for a duration of 55 years, renewable by tacit agreement.[5] This is a period equivalent to the very existence of the Senegal state.

In both cases, the lands in question are inhabited and used by communities that identify themselves as belonging to the Fulani (or Fulɓe) group, present throughout West Africa and traditionally dedicated to the breeding of zebu cattle (also known as Peul zebu) as well as other animals such as goats, sheep and donkeys (Dupire, 1962).[6] In fact, the Senegal River Valley, as well as the delta occupying its westernmost part, covers a semi-arid territory included in the Sahelian climate belt, where semi-extensive livestock breeding activities, especially grazing and transhumance, are still widespread, at least as mixed agro-pastoral practices. Such activities have clearly had a decisive impact in characterizing the history of the region and defined how pastoral populations relate to land in terms of property rights, access and use. They have also contributed to the peripheral and marginal position, both geographically and socially, of these populations in the broader context of the historical evolutions and political-economic development of the Senegalese state and society.

The investors' arrival has been a dramatic event for the pastoral communities that inhabit the land leased to the Italian company. Not only are the two approaches, both based on extensive land use, de facto incompatible, but the agricultural project is to be carried out on, and overlaps with, the living and domestic space of the villagers inhabiting the Ndiaël Avifauna Reserve, making real coexistence impossible. This is the situation at the origin of a conflict that lasted about four years and was only interrupted by the company's bankruptcy, and that is, however, still latent.

A wetland of international importance

Situated in the south-east of the delta region about 50 kilometres from the city of Saint Louis, the Ndiaël Reserve, or Ndiaël Avifauna Reserve, as it has been renamed since the 1990s, is home to the largest expanse of land not reserved for agriculture in the delta. Before its partial downsizing in 2012, the reserve was about 46,500 hectares, between the national road and the western shore of Lake Guiers (see Figure 0.1). The area owes its name to a large depression area (*cuvette*) called Ndiaël, which covers about 10,000 hectares. Located in the northern part, it has the shape of an oval with the major axis stretching in a north-east/south-east direction for about 15 kilometres, while the minor axis is approximately 8.5 kilometres (Humbert et al, 1995). Like other depressions in the delta, the Ndiaël regularly received water from the Senegal River, which flooded periodically. The flooding began between July and August, during the dry season, and reached a depth of 1.5 metres in the middle of the *cuvette* around October. Thereafter, the water level gradually decreased until the next flood, but never completely disappeared. Sometimes, as many as 30,000 hectares could be impacted by the flood, as happened in the 1950s when the nearby town of Richard Toll was totally submerged.

Because of slow water drainage and the highly impermeable nature of the soil, the Ndiaël was an important wetland, characterized by vegetation consisting mainly of annual grasses highly resistant to drought and an important component of cattle diets. The Ndiaël also attracted a large and varied fauna, including freshwater boars, monitor lizards, monkeys, hyenas and rabbits. Many of these animals, albeit in smaller numbers, can still be seen today. The most distinctive presence, however, is that of birds, especially aquatic ones, including both African and migratory species from northern Europe for which, in particular, Ndiaël is an important stop. Towards the end of the 1950s, the construction of the RN2 national road (from Saint Louis to the town of Rosso on the Senegal–Mauritania border) and, subsequently, of several dams placed on its main tributaries, resulted in the isolation of the depression from the seasonal water flow, causing it to progressively dry out. Today, the landscape resembles a vast desert whose end is difficult to imagine. The dry land has sparse and thinning vegetation, and in several areas the soil is white, covered with salt encrustations. The depression can be driven through during the dry season. However, it is only possible to cross it along a few well-trodden paths and care must be taken not to go off the track because, despite the desert-like appearance of its surface, the ground underneath is soaked with water and vehicles risk sinking into it.

The soils of the Ndiaël depression have a high clay component and, for this reason, they are almost impermeable and strongly allomorphic with respect to the context; they are also high in salinity. It was precisely owing to these pedological characteristics that the depression was spared from the agricultural conversion that was affecting other delta depressions in the early 1960s. The Fulani groups that travelled through the reserve, and made camp there, gained access from the north or the south, and would bypass the depression in order to allow their animals to graze. Here, the sandy, elevated lands provided important pastures during the rainy season, while the flooded lands near Lake Guiers provided fertile soils conducive to agriculture. The latter have been excluded from the reserve and now host the fields of local farmers.

As for the part extending south-west of the Ndiaël *cuvette*, in the direction of Lake Guiers and continuing towards the rural community of Keur Moumar Sarr, it consists mainly of sandy soils with moderately rugged relief, which is covered with a dense and varied grassy carpet during the rainy season. The landscape is also marked by a thinning shrub steppe that includes some fruit trees, several species of acacias, baobabs and other plants typical of the Sahelian savannahs. The vast sandy expanses are in turn interspersed with depression-clay zones, capable of collecting rainwater, which creates a series of small temporary ponds: *weendo*, from their name in *Pulaar*, which can provide water for two to three months a year before drying up completely. Here, both the texture of the soil and the vegetation are different, with tree species that cannot be found elsewhere in the rest of the delta. Finally, in some places, the reserve has more barren parts composed of lateritic-ferruginous soils where the vegetation is very sparse.

The creation of the protected area by decree in 1965,[7] just three years after Senegal's independence, with the decision to classify this area as a special reserve, was intended as compensation, as clarified in the text of the law, for the previous allocation of two other areas for agricultural exploitation: the former partial fauna reserve of Djeuss (56,000 hectares)[8] and Boundoum (27,000 hectares), whose classification most likely dated back to colonial times. These areas, totalling 83,000 hectares, represented two of the largest flood zones in the delta. The classification as a reserve, however, in no way contemplated the preservation, care and support of pastoral practices and of the local villages. The same classification decree authorizes the use of the forest for grazing activities on traditional paths as well as the collection of fruit and dry branches but prohibits the settlement of villages and does not deal with the increase in population which, in the case of pastoral communities, implies not so much a widening of settlements but rather a fractioning and a wider scattering in the territory, with the development of new settlements.

These are important elements that will make the living conditions of the Ndiaël people ever more precarious. When the delta lands were given to local communities to manage in 1972, with the task of allocating them to residents, the villagers in the reserve found themselves excluded from this land distribution process, as they could not claim any rights to forest land. They could not even apply for title to the land that had been developed in the meantime and become owners of their own homes. Incidentally, such an approach was in line with the environmental conservation discipline of the time and with the Senegalese Forest Code. Without changing much of its spirit, this code reformed the previous colonial legislation regulated by the decree of 4 July 1935 on the French West African forest regime. If the French law had a repressive approach, basically oriented towards 'protecting the forests from their inhabitants', the subsequent Senegalese texts considered the local populations as subjects not to be involved in the management of resources, as they did not have any legitimate property rights, with the exception of a few rights of use that nevertheless represented a step forward compared to the colonial approach.

In 1998, Senegal also reformed its forestry code (*Loi n° 98-164 du 20 février 1998 portant code forestier*), replacing that of 1965, and introduced a distinction between reserves, special reserves and sylvo-pastoral reserves. While in the latter herders are authorized to set up temporary camps necessary for family life (Article 4), this is not the case for special reserves such as the Ndiaël Avifauna Reserve. These are in fact defined as 'areas where, for scientific, tourist or ecological reasons, certain temporary or permanent restrictions are necessary on hunting, fishing, the capture of animals, the exploitation of plants, soil and subsoil products or the construction of infrastructures for scientific, tourist or ecological purposes' (Article 7).

From Europe to Senegal, the long migration of environmental protection regulations

According to what we have been able to reconstruct, the decision to grant a special regime for the Ndiaël depression was most probably also supported by the consensus of the Conseil international de la Chasse et de la conservation du gibier (CIC; International Council for Game and Wildlife Conservation), whose headquarters are in Paris, but which has a number of affiliated associations in the delta, whose intervention in the Ndiaël, with the aim of preservation and ecological restoration, has been witnessed since the 1970s. The reserve is also an important territory for the CIC: the migratory birds that are hunted in Europe and therefore need this space to arrive alive on the continent commute here. The CIC's interest in the preservation of wetlands is also rooted in the relationship that historically links hunting activities to these ecosystems, which are now among the main places dedicated to this activity. In France, it was under the *ancien régime* that the special relationship between hunting and wetlands was established following the exclusion of the latter from the nascent regulations, which, by not legislating on them, essentially ended up giving them the character of *hors-la-loi* territories (Derex, 2001). This made them available to the poorer groups who practised hunting activities that were defined as 'poor' because they only involved certain types of game and were not permitted in the remaining territory (Estève, 2006).

Hardly workable or arable, these lands also became the preferred sites for pastoralism (see also Moriceau, 1999). As was the case in the delta, wetlands in France were also considered useless, residual areas for a long time, until about the 1970s: worthless sources of diseases, they received little consideration, even by planners. In this sense, the Ndiaël Reserve allows us to build a link with the events that involved the inhabitants of wetlands in Europe, and especially in France, in their relations with the monarchic classes first and with the advent of bourgeois society later, in turn inscribed in the evolution of relations between private interests and common needs, between the countryside and the city. Indeed, part of the complexity of interpreting the conflict under scrutiny precisely concerns its relationship with the colonial experience that produced the transfer to the African continent of the French system's own classification and interpretation of river and wetland areas.

The direct intervention of the CIC in favour of the establishment of the reserve does not appear in any official document.[9] However, it would explain the attention devoted to the Ndiaël depression at a time when the importance of the ecosystem services provided by these habitats had not been fully recognized yet. For this to happen, it was in fact necessary to wait until 1971, when the Ramsar Convention on Wetlands of International Importance Especially as Waterfowl Habitat, whose partnership also included the CIC, was signed. Article 7 of the reserve's classification decree already mentioned the need to restore the ecological functions of the *cuvette* through its '*remise en eau*'. The decree provided for the subsequent issue of a document containing specific provisions for such operations. However, there is no trace of this document, but in 1977 Senegal was one of the first states, and the first West African country, to become a party to the Ramsar Convention, which covers the 10,000 hectares of the Ndiaël *cuvette*, ranked 139th.

Because of its progressive degradation, in 1995 the Ndiaël area was also included in the Montreux register of ecologically degraded wetlands.[10] In 1991, within the framework of this convention, the CIC also financed the first feasibility study for the restoration of Ndiaël's normal flooding cycle. The restoration of the depression's ecological functions was to become a *leitmotiv* of development cooperation in the area, and a series of ecological restoration projects have interested the area from its declaration as a Montreux site until today. However, despite the many programmes implemented to restore water supply, problems persist, and ecosystem degradation increases annually. It was within the framework of one of these interventions, namely the Projet d'Aménagement et de Développement du Ndiaël (PADIN; Ndiaël Integrated Planning and Development Project) , created in 1997, that the division of the reserve into three zones first appeared: *tampon*, *cuvette* and *périphérique*, as we now know it. The *cuvette* corresponds to the 10,000 hectares of the depression, surrounded by a further 10,000 hectares of the 'buffer zone' which, in turn, are part of a 26,500-hectare 'peripheral zone'. It was this latter that was downgraded and granted to the Senhuile-Senethanol group.

To understand this decision, it is important to consider how, even though the decree prevented their agricultural exploitation, these lands have also historically and politically been frontier areas from the point of view of the Senegalese state and the various development actors interested in expanding irrigated agriculture in the region. Moreover, attempts to make the reserve arable are not new. As early as 1967, a study commissioned by the Institute for Tropical Agricultural Research and Food Crops proposed using the Ndiaël area as a basin to accommodate rice drainage water, provided it was not too salty.[11] A 1995 study bemoans the persistence and reiteration of this hypothesis (Humbert et al, 1995), while Jean-François Tourrand (2000, p 76) writes that the connection of Ndiaël with the nearby Kassak, an outflowing stream of the Senegal River, caused the contamination of the depression flooded with agricultural residual water. Although the first idea was shelved, the prospect of an agricultural conversion of the reserve was again put forward within the framework of the Programme de développement des marchés agricoles du Sénégal (PDMAS; Agricultural Markets and Agribusiness Development Project for Senegal) presented by the Senegalese state in collaboration with the World Bank and approved in 2007.

With respect to all this, the start of the Senhuile-Senethanol project, although representing a new factor inscribed in a contemporary global dynamic, is consistent with the recent history of this territory and makes it possible to highlight its contradictions and limitations. The whole affair highlights the progressive weakening of its historical inhabitants' right of stay, but also, as we shall see, the role of pastoralism in the more general context of the delta. Having been designated a nature reserve, this area has, over the years, represented an important shelter for pastoralism, gradually pushed out by agricultural development. The presence of villages has always been tolerated and included in the management plans of rural communities, albeit with various limitations. In 2011, a year before the forest was downgraded and granted to Senhuile-Senethanol, the villagers of Bellel Mbamby, which means 'small donkey pond' in Pulaar, had asked the Service des Eaux et Forêts [Directorate of Water and Forestry] permission to exploit this resource to irrigate a small field for fodder. This action testifies to the progressive desire to introduce other feeding systems alongside transhumance. Initially, the ban on cultivation had not greatly worried the villages, which in any case were not interested in this activity or had other land at their disposal (on the banks of the lake or on the edges of the reserve). Today, however, this limitation is starting to raise concerns. The reduction of grazing land forces local herders to make up for the lack of resources, and the opportunity to combine transhumance with on-site fodder cultivation is of increasing interest to them.

The authorities gave a negative response and did not fail to mention that the very presence of the village on the territory was to be considered 'irregular'. Yet the residents of the reserve are the most directly involved in its preservation; in fact, in 2003, the 'Biodiversity Project: Senegal-Mauritania',

Figure 1.1: Water and biodiversity in the Ndiaël Reserve (1)

Note: One of the temporary ponds that form in the clay areas of the Ndiaël Reserve during the rainy season and remain for many months during the dry season, constituting an important source of water for the villages and fauna of the reserve. At the bottom right of the photo, you can glimpse women washing clothes.

Source: Author

Figure 1.2: Water and biodiversity in the Ndiaël Reserve (2)

Note: Grazing cows refresh themselves at a pond in Ndiaël during the dry season. Not visible, behind the trees, in the background, is a more desert-like area, interspersed only by a few baobabs and shrubs, which will be covered with a thick tuft of grass when the rains start.

Source: Author

aimed at promoting a participatory approach to the management of the site, established the Association Inter-villageoise (AIV; Inter-village Association), which is committed to the preservation of biodiversity and has 800 members, all from the 32 official villages located in the reserve. The AIV has benefited from other projects and funding in collaboration with international associations such as the US Millennium Challenge Corporation and the World Bank, promoting respectively the Senegal Compact and the Integrated Marine and Coastal Resources Management Project (GRIMAC), as well as the International Union for Conservation of Nature (IUCN) and Wetlands International Africa (WIA). The latter, a branch of the non-governmental organization Wetland International, a member of the United Nations Educational, Scientific and Cultural Organization, after strongly opposing Senhuile's investment with a view to supporting resident populations, had signed an agreement with the company to collaborate on rehabilitation activities in the area. Although this event aroused the indignation of the populations, it is consistent from the organization's point of view. Its core mission is in fact the preservation of the wetland and therefore of the *cuvette*, an opportunity that does not seem to be incompatible a priori with the agricultural use of surrounding areas. According to the United Nations, 2014 was also the year of family farming, and the Ramsar Convention launched the slogan 'Wetlands and Agriculture, Partners for Growth' as the theme of the activities held on World Wetlands Day (2 February). On the Convention's website and printed posters, the photo illustrating this slogan shows a water basin surrounded by a huge sunflower field.

Ecology and politics of pastoralism in the Senegal River delta

Closer to the semantic field of subalternity, the notion of marginality introduces the idea of an otherness that is given as an outcome of and in opposition to the dynamics of exclusion. In the context we are discussing, it also suggests the idea of a physical-spatial positioning with respect to power. The history of pastoralism in the Senegal River delta region seems to respond particularly well to this further specification. Here, historically, pastoral mobility and the structures of command and self-government typical of nomadic and semi-nomadic Sahelian societies have tended to result in the physical distancing from large territorial powers.[12] The idea of marginality and marginalization associated with these societies went hand in hand with that of periphery and distance from central power. This strategy, however, clashed with the progressive agricultural colonization of the area.

The farming communities have had to face the socio-economic evolutions that have taken place in the region, starting from a twofold condition of disadvantage. Poorly understood, if not stigmatized altogether, in their productive rationality by national agricultural policies and substantially ignored by land policies, they have also been put in a subordinate position in terms of development choices and trajectories at a regional level. According to local policies, in the absence of real support and lacking significant grazing land, herding communities were forced to choose between agriculture, agro-pastoralism (centred on rice farming) and livestock farming. It is from this position of marginality that these same people were faced with a conflict in which they oppose the logic of capitalist valorization and appropriation, on a global scale, for which their land represents a frontier on several levels.

A historically pastoral region

Located in the extreme west of the Senegal River Valley in the north of the country, the river delta also covers Mauritanian territories. Historically disputed between the powers of neighbouring empires, the area coincides almost entirely with the ancient kingdom of Waalo, a basin of Wolof domination (circa 13th century to 1858) (Barry, 2014). The Senegalese part of the delta designates a natural region covering approximately 5,000 square kilometres,[13] generally divided into upper, middle and lower delta. Lake Guiers, which bounds the area to the east, is the largest source of fresh water in Senegal and the main water supply for the city of Dakar. Unlike with the ocean to the west and the river to the north, the southern limits of the delta are not well defined. They are marked by the beginning of the vast semi-desert expanse that formed a large part of the ancient kingdom of Cayor (1549–1886) and can be imagined as a line running parallel to the Saint Louis-Rosso road, about 10 kilometres to the south.

Due to the low rainfall,[14] the delta definitely has a Sahelian climate, with an average temperature fluctuating between 20 and 40 degrees centigrade and an annual cycle marked by three major macro-seasons: *hivernage* or rainy season (July to September), dry-cold season (October to March) and dry-warm season (April to July). In addition to temperature and rainfall intensity, the vegetation is also influenced by river floods and salt intrusion from sea water into the Senegal River, resulting in its salinization. The flood begins in June near the town of Bakkel, at the other end of the valley, and reaches the delta in July where it peaks around November. This period also coincides with the swelling of the river caused by the arrival of water from the ocean, which infiltrates about 200 kilometres upstream to recede in August, nine months later.

Before the infrastructural interventions carried out by the Senegalese government, the two phenomena just described – the flood and salt intrusion – each involved the filling of the distributaries that form the delta's rich hydrographic system. Their subsequent overflow generated the flooding and salinization of the depression areas near the rivers, called *waalo*, as opposed to the dune zones, far from the river, called *jeeri*, untouched by the floods. Once the flood was over, the current reversed and the waters that had not yet evaporated flowed back into the river. This opposition between *waalo* and *jeeri* lands is typical of the entire Senegal River Valley, generally structured on a north-east (*waalo*)/south-west (*jeeri*) spatial axis. While maintaining this division in general terms, the pedological organization of the delta is organized less schematically; here the *waalo* and *jeeri* zones are interspersed in a more haphazard manner. However, it is possible to define an approximate boundary of the two lands, marked by the highway, which connects Saint Louis to the town of Rosso Sénégal (see Figure 0.1). To the north of this, where the main watercourses flow, there are more *waalo* lands, while extending inland to the south there are the *jeeri* savannah expanses.

In addition to the *waalo–jeeri* separation, a further distinction, used locally, classifies soils based on their composition and in relation to their distance and height above sea and river level. The *waalo* includes the clayey depression soils called *hollades*, which are flooded regularly. The *jeeri* soils, untouched by river floods and mostly located in what is called the *arrière-pays*, have different characteristics according to altitude and composition. Up to the RN2 national road, and slightly further south, are the red dunes formed in the Ogolian dry phase (between 25,000 and 13,000 years ago), aligned longitudinally in an east/south-west direction, below which lie the plateaus with brown-sandy or lateritic soils. The delta lands are also characterized by the intensity of their salinity levels. More pronounced in the *waalo* lands, salinity represents a problem common to the whole region and affects the entire water table. The high salt content is an obstacle to irrigation by wells, which is particularly problematic in the *jeeri* lands, given their distance from the river.

Due to the combination of the characteristics mentioned so far – the salinity of the soils, the intensity of the floods, their duration and the time of year when they occurred – the delta, unlike the rest of the valley, was hardly suitable for dry or floodplain farming (Tourrand, 2000). This kind of agriculture was normally practised, throughout the entire Senegal River Valley, in the depression ponds located on clay soil near the river following the withdrawal of water during the dry season. In the case of the delta, however, only the riverbanks lent themselves to cultivation, and only for the few months of the year when they were not reached by floods. Poorly suited to agriculture, this land has nevertheless historically defined itself as an optimal region for the development of itinerant and extensive pastoralism, practised in particular by groups of Fulani herders. The transhumance cycles were mostly organized along trajectories from the *waalo* lands to the *jeeri* lands and vice versa. Together, these two areas provided diverse pastures capable of maintaining a high animal load with an average of one beast per hectare throughout the year (Audru, 1996). The hollow lands of the *waalo*, unsuitable for agricultural purposes as they were submerged most of the year, became accessible as the rains stopped, providing rich fodder associated with an abundant supply of fresh water. The growing plants absorbed salt, a key element in the cattle diet, from the soil.

The *waalo* was therefore an important resource which allowed livestock to survive the harsh dry season of Sahelian climates, but it also offered species suitable for human consumption which are still praised in traditional local songs to this day. When, because of river floods, the *waalo* became impassable and the entire area was reduced to a swamp difficult to cross that attracted wild beasts and mosquitoes, it was the *jeeri*, the site of temporary *hivernage* camps (*rumano* in Pulaar), which, grown green again thanks to the rains that had come in the meantime, became essential to feed the herds. It also allowed for the integration of cattle farming with rainfed farming of millet and other plants. Micro- and macro-movements were organized according to a pastoral calendar that, unlike the division adopted so far (rains, and two dry seasons), was based on the alternation of five different seasons.

The walking of cattle was also facilitated by the low population density, which allowed the herds great freedom of movement. In contrast, the *Moyen delta* in the interior was practically empty, as it was a vast swamp most of the time; only the herders entered it (Hervouët, 1971). In addition to the Fulani herders–farmers, a few Wolof villagers lived on the banks of the river or on the southern *waalo–jeeri* edge, where they cultivated millet (with both rainfed and floodplain farming), sometimes combined with fishing. From the early 20th century onwards, we also find the villages of Haratine people, freed slaves, also engaged in pastoralism (Tourrand et al, 1985).

The presence of herders in the delta was highly mobile. According to Christian Santoir, a more substantial settlement of Fulani groups in the delta coincided with the French colonial expansion (Santoir, 1977). However, although colonization and the creation of the *contoir* of Saint Louis had developed a trade network with the Waalo kingdom, helping to increase its power, the natural limitations presented by the delta ecosystem meant that the demography in its interior areas remained relatively unchanged. In 1955, the territory as a whole had about 11,000 inhabitants (Tourrand et al, 1985) and, according to the data reported in J. Audru's well-organized study (1996, p 181), in the year 1964, the rural population was around 17,000, with an average density of five inhabitants per square kilometre.

With the start of the hydraulic territorialization works initiated by the new Senegalese state, the situation just described underwent a drastic change that would deeply revolutionize the social, political and environmental balance of the region. In fact, it was only from the 1950s that the colonial project for the agricultural exploitation of the delta took hold, thanks to more consistent interventions aimed at regulating the level and duration of floods, which would continue in independent Senegal until the 1990s. The development of irrigation agriculture through the creation of agricultural perimeters in large depressions would later also lead to the displacement of pastoralist populations, preventing their access to water and making the sustainability of pastoralism in the region ever more precarious. The emphasis on agriculture as the basis for the development of an independent Senegal state and access to land through agricultural cooperatives reinforced the disavowal of pastoralists' land rights in both Senegalese legislation and customary practices. In the following years, the reorganization of space, conveyed by hydraulic works and land segmentation, would also contribute to creating new social relations and hierarchies of belonging, interfering with local land uses, modifying the landscape and its biological conformation.

Water more than land: agricultural colonization of the delta

In 1964, the construction of an 82-kilometre-long dam on the Senegalese side of the river, financed by major development banks, and supplemented by a series of other small dams located at multiple tributaries, caused the normal flood cycles to stop. As a result, 30,000 hectares of low-lying areas, some of the best pastures in the dry season, became isolated and were no longer filled with water as regularly as they used to be. Herders were not only deprived of access to land, but also to river water. In most of the perimeter areas, the passage of herds was formally forbidden in order to protect crops (Hervouët, 1971).

Tourrand (2000) estimates that the first round of hydraulic interventions in the delta resulted in a 70 per cent reduction of pastoral space in the *waalo*. Even in the areas spared by agricultural conversion, the infrastructural interventions had disrupted the normal water supply, causing faster drainage with consequent drying of the rain ponds and reduction of fodder resources (Diagne, 1974). The dams were supposed to prevent salt water from overflowing, allowing the river water to drain away during only two to three months of non-saline flooding. However, when salinity rose from underground, most of the land became impassable and in the first years of the project's implementation Senegal managed to ensure the transformation of only four agricultural perimeters for a total of 9,100 hectares, which would rise to 14,000 in 1990 with the addition of other perimeters, all concentrated in the upper part of the delta (Tourrand, 2000, p 43). Technical and environmental problems made production erratic and weak, requiring another round of planning in the mid-1960s to make irrigation and flooding more regular and predictable.

In order to understand why development was destined to fail in the delta, it is important to consider it against the planning rationale of that period, in which concepts such as scarcity and underdevelopment went hand in hand with an environmental determinism that concealed the ecological component of planning and considered space as an abstract component on which to plan freely (Quatrida, 2012). According to such a vision, any kind of territorial persistence could be interpreted as a disturbance and, on a sociological level, it turned into the need for modernization, with a view to abandoning tradition in search of other forms of rationality and innovations. The delta was not the only river area in the Sahel in which a process of hetero-directed hydraulic territorialization was initiated by resorting to massive investments and infrastructural interventions (Woodhouse et al, 2000). Once again, it is worth recalling that all this followed in the wake of the colonial development approach that had attempted on several occasions to make the delta an important source of agricultural raw materials, particularly as a response to the decline of the slave trade economy. The technique of controlled flooding had also been introduced in Africa by the French colony, with an initial application in the Niger delta, based on what had already been experimented in the Mêkong delta region, which today is the most important and largest rice-producing area in Vietnam.

The first attempts by the colonial authorities to implement irrigation techniques in Senegal dated back to 1821 and they were aimed at the production of sugar cane, cotton and indigo. It was at that time that, following an agreement signed between the *brack* (the authority) of the Waalo kingdom and the then governor of the colony, France obtained the assignment of the kingdom's lands (Tourrand, 2000). The impossibility to effectively control the lands, the political instability of the region plagued by conflicts with neighbouring peoples, combined with the less than encouraging results on a technical-agricultural level, led the colony to opt for peanut production in the centre-east of the country and Saint Louis once again became a commercial hub, centred on the trade of rubber obtained from the acacias that grow abundantly in the Sahelian savannahs. It was only at the end of the First World War that France resumed irrigation projects for cultivation in the delta, driven in part by the decrease in rice imports guaranteed by French Indochina and needed to feed the settlers in the cities. In 1946, a new experiment was attempted at Richard Toll. It started with 600 hectares and reached 6,000 hectares in 1955; three years later, the Richard Toll *colonat* was created to house the immigrants arriving from Europe. Grouped into cooperatives, the settlers were contractually committed to devote themselves solely to rice cultivation. Parallel to this, the first attempts to regulate the duration and intensity of flooding to cultivate the *waalo* began.

With independence, the project was taken over by the Société nationale d'aménagement et d'exploitation des terres du delta du fleuve Sénégal (SAED; Senegal River Delta Land Development and Exploitation Company),[15] which intervened in the delta thanks to the passing of legislation that had allowed it to be declared 'pioneer land', a category that could be attributed to lands defined as residual and suitable for development plans.[16] In order to cultivate the rice fields, SAED organized the immigration of 9,000 families from different parts of the country and five new villages were built. This was the beginning of a growing demographic expansion, which was also a consequence of the gradual settlement of inhabitants who traditionally occupied a small space for a limited period of the year. Population density in the delta rose from five inhabitants per square kilometre in 1964 to 21 inhabitants in 1970 (Hervouët, 1971). This growth was the precondition for a hitherto non-existent land conflict (Audru, 1996) that was mainly characterized by the opposition between farmers and herders.

This conflict was exacerbated in the 1970s and 1980s in conjunction with the process of liberalization of development and the administrative reform of 1975, which sanctioned the change of the delta from *zone pionnière* to *zone de terroir*. Land management would henceforth no longer be the responsibility of the government, but it would be entrusted to the rural communities. As a consequence, between 1981 and 1983, following the law enforcement decree, the delta experienced a veritable land rush that led to land being allocated to non-residents or non-farmers (traders and religious authorities, state officials or former employees of the Compagnie Sucrière Sénégalaise [Senegalese Sugar Company]) (Mathieu et al, 1989). Most of the successful applications from farmers in the area mostly belonged to the *aristocratie paysanne*: village chiefs, presidents of cooperatives and their relatives (Mathieu et al, 1989).

In general, throughout the 1980s and 1990s, the number of private perimeters (ranging from 5 to 100 hectares) increased exponentially, exceeding in volume the areas irrigated by the state. This is the period that herders ironically call the 'walking of the fields', in opposition to the current expression 'walking of the cattle' used to denounce the lack of control of the cows walking on cultivated fields. Irrigated agricultural land increased from 10,386 hectares in 1980 (SAED, 1990) to about 28,865 hectares in 1991, of which about 15,000 belong to private perimeters.[17] At the turn of the year 2000, agricultural land in the delta covered approximately 44,000 hectares (SAED, 2011).

Pastoral trajectories in the delta

It would be a mistake to think of pastoralists as helpless victims of the changes affecting them. Gradually excluded from the most fertile lands close to water, the Fulani farmers have opted for different adaptation strategies. Some families have decided to implement the same land accumulation techniques adopted by the groups that traditionally practised agriculture, in order to preserve their traditional rights over the land now set aside for rice-growing, seeking to become tributaries of a perimeter, not without

Figure 1.3: Agricultural expansion in the Senegal River delta, 1960s to early 2000s

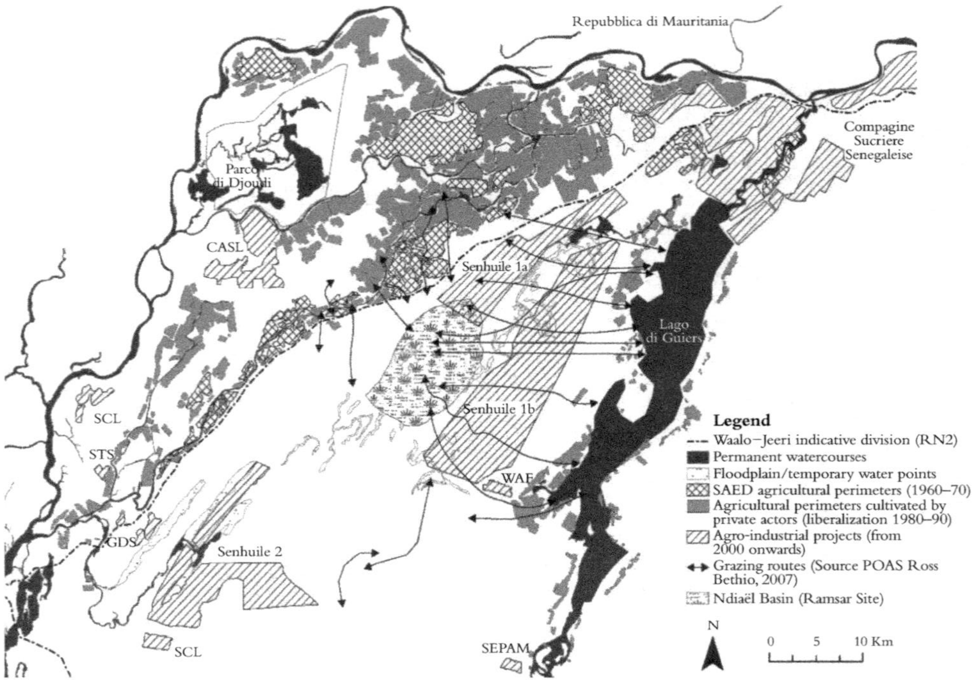

Note: Expansion of agricultural cultivation and reductions in grazing areas in the Senegal delta from the 1960s to the early 2000s based on data collected in February 2014. Agricultural, state and private perimeters located in the *waalo* part, above the line representing the RN2 national road, can be seen. In contrast, the majority of recent private investments are located in the so-called *arrière pays*, a fallback zone of extensive pastoralism, on the edge of the region. The area pertaining to the Senhuile project, shown on the map, corresponds to the cultivated and/or deforested areas as revealed by GPS surveys carried out in February 2014. An additional area assigned to Senhuile in the delta is also indicated, in addition to the Ndiaël Reserve, located in the Fass Ngom Rural Community and whose current concession status is unknown.

Source: Benegiamo and Cirillo (2016, p 128)

conflict or rivalry with the Wolof groups. The traditional complementarity between flood farming and pastoralism has been replaced by a particular form of agro-pastoralism centred on rice cultivation, which presents different levels of integration between the two activities, going as far as the complete '*agriculturization*' of herders, with their conversion into a sedentary population. However, the opposite phenomenon can also be observed that tends towards the separation of agriculture and animal husbandry. This is especially the case for those herders who are predominantly and traditionally settled on *jeeri* lands and who, having chosen to maintain their specialization or not having been able to claim some form of belonging on the lands and paths close to the river, have not been able to benefit from the agricultural attributions in the *waalo*.

In order to understand the persistence of pastoralism in the delta, however, it is also important to situate it in the broader Sahelian context within which this practice takes place. The term Sahel designates a long strip of territory that crosses the African continent from east to west, extending over 13 states in sub-Saharan Africa, from the Atlantic Ocean to the Red Sea. Its place name derives from the Arabic word *sahil* (ساحل), the 'shore', and has expressed, since antiquity, the idea of a threshold. An arrival point for Africa's long caravans before heading out into the great sea of desert, the Sahel covers a transition zone that stretches over some 3,000,000 square kilometres, separating the great Saharan expanses to the north from the pluvial vegetation of the forest-savannah to the south. Commonly divided into three sub-zones – North Sahel, Sahel 'proper' and South Sahel – it is a region that, as written by geographer Jean Gallais (1984), is deeply marked by aridity although it is not a completely desert area. With its three months of rainfall and an average rainfall rate of around 400 mm per year (ranging from 150 mm to 600 mm), this uneven and geographically complex landscape is characterized by the presence of numerous herds that spend most of their time in search of pasture, moving along seasonal paths.

Cattle farming is a dominant activity in these territories; itinerant and extensive pastoralism involves between 70 and 90 per cent of the Sahelian herds (Touré et al, 2012). However, it is improper to speak of pastoralism in the Sahel in the singular, given the variety of pastoral modes practised here, among which transhumant, nomadic, agro-pastoral. Historically inscribed in the social structures of a territory whose fodder supply is enriched by the presence of numerous allogenic rivers and important wetlands, today, with over 60 million head of cattle and 160 million small ruminants, the Sahel remains a land of cattle farming par excellence (ECOWAS, 2008). This activity accounts for up to 40 per cent of the agricultural gross domestic product of the economies of Sahelian West African countries (ECOWAS, 2008).

An 'eco-dynamic' practice

The importance of different pastoral practices in this context cannot be attributed solely to the value of tradition and custom. Firstly because, despite its conservative traits, pastoral practice has never ceased to change in order to deal with the social, political and climatic evolutions to which it is exposed. Secondly, because pastoralism is a mode of production capable of optimally organizing the circulation, distribution and consumption of resources in specific ecological contexts that tend to be inhospitable, such as the semi-arid climates of Sahelian lands. Its effectiveness in transforming the sparse plant cover that characterizes the Sahelian savannahs into food (meat, milk and dairies), fibres (leather and textiles) and services needed to survive and develop under extreme ecological conditions makes pastoralism a strategic activity in Sahelian territories characterized by general aridity and recurrent drought (Nori et al, 2008). From a pastoral point of view, seasonal transhumance represents the way in which livestock density can be regulated on grazing routes, thus preventing their degradation. The walking of different animal species – cows, sheep, goats, dromedaries – also makes it possible to fully exploit the plant biodiversity of the routes. These aspects, combined with the flexibility of pastoral routes, have proven to be a highly suitable technique for managing the risks and the many uncertainties to which Sahelian societies are exposed.[18]

In addition to being an ecological necessity, mobility over an extensive area therefore offers economic advantages. Comparative studies (see, for instance, Colin de Verdière, 1995) carried out on different herds in the Filingué region, in Niger, still within the Sahelian area, have shown how mobility positively affects milk production, which is one of the main commercial products, confirming what herders have already asserted. Finally, pastoralism plays a fundamental role in the savings strategies of Sahelian rural economies where having a good stock of cattle may prove to be the only winning strategy in case of drought or difficult years. Moreover, in periods marked by low rainfall, itinerant grazing systems survive better than more fixed or sedentary ones. After all, the advantage of owning a mobile asset (herds) over an immobile asset (land) is linked precisely to the ability of the former to move and chase the randomness of rainfall.

Despite this, pastoralism has for a long time continued to be treated, both in scientific-academic circles and in the context of public policy and development, as a predatory and high-impact activity as far as resources and the environment are concerned, responsible for phenomena such as soil degradation and advancing desertification. The disavowal of mobility and of the social-cultural and cost-saving value of livestock was largely based on a view of pastoralism as an irrational, unprofessional, economically unproductive practice that needed to be modernized (Santoir, 1983).

Transhumance then took on the appearance of backward and simplistic expedients to cope with climatic risks. In line with this reasoning, herders have also long been pointed out as the main culprits of their own poverty.[19] Consequently, the various development programmes focused their efforts on making pastoralist systems more profitable, promoting the sedentarization of herders and increased marketing of livestock, or directly converting their land to agriculture, which was seen as a practice more in line with national economic development.

In Senegal, where the last census in 2005 counted approximately 2,900,000 cattle (Cesaro et al, 2010) and where ruminant (cattle, sheep and goat) farming covers the entire country, constituting the main source of income for more than 350,000 households (around 6 per cent of the country's gross domestic product) (Castañeda, 2005) this perception is rooted in the colonial view of pastoral practice. This is mainly because the colonial administration – whose only interest was its potential role as a supplier of meat for urban markets – favoured an approach to the sector focused on improving animal health. The only possible aim in that context was to increase the number of head, but this implied the transformation of pastoralists into 'economic actors' interested in developing trade (Landais, 1990). This objective was pursued by resorting to veterinary medicine on the one hand and through attempts to promote pastoral sedentariness on the other. In addition, a system of taxation per head of livestock was introduced, which ended up encouraging herders to move away from control centres.

Independent Senegal retained the modernist approach, and the new policies have perpetuated the same health objectives, aimed at marketing animals for the supply of cheap meat in urban markets and controlling or reducing the mobility of herders. As proof of this, it can be pointed out that the first ministry to deal with the administration of livestock breeding (Ministère de l'élevage [Minisry of Livestock]) was only established in 1998, which collaborated with the already existing Direction de l'élevage [Directorate of Livestock]. On the other hand, the vision of the pastoralists living in straw huts, surrounded by numerous and valuable animals, unable to transform them into wealth that they could take advantage of, contributed to the image of pastoralism as an irrational and uneconomic practice, making the herders guilty of keeping for themselves – and wasting – a capital that, like the land, should belong to the nation.

In fact, as Santoir points out in his studies on the delta region (Santoir, 1983), the mention of sedentarization never explicitly appears in the first texts produced for Senegalese development policies and programmes and, rather, it is imagined and results as a kind of expected effect. For instance, this is the purpose of the creation of a series of wells in the Ferlo region, an extremely arid area south of the Senegal River Valley, and the subsequent organization into 'pastoral units' of the various camps established within its surroundings. Towards the end of the 1980s, these were followed by the creation of the sylvo-pastoral reserves that perpetuated the territorial zoning at the basis of an attempt to organize the country. These practices, including the creation of wells, which are still promoted in many arid and semi-arid areas, are often strongly opposed by the pastoralists themselves because they lead to a concentration of cattle and the unification of pastoral routes, resulting in increased environmental pressure and thus ecosystem degradation, including an increased incidence of disease for the animals, which are gathered in herds that are too big.

Understanding and bias in public policy

This overly technical approach and lack of understanding of pastoral logic thus illustrate the wrong assumptions these policies are based on, which involve the disavowal of the herders' role in land management as well as the strategic importance of a practice strongly centred on mobility and on the search for a delicate balance between resources and space. Moreover, it was not until at least the 1990s that pastoralism became the subject of a partial scientific reappraisal. It is above all the debate on *range-lands* in the context of the so-called 'new range ecology' that has contributed to redefining the terms of the analysis for understanding the functioning of arid and semi-arid territories in general, and of grazing areas in particular (Westoby et al, 1999). Most of these studies – initially focused on the ecological balance of the great steppes of the United States that host important grazing activities – have challenged the idea that these areas respond to a principle of static balance, highlighting in fact the existence of dynamic ecological logics. The result was an understanding of pastoral lands as subject to endogenous processes of desertification and regeneration driven by abiotic and stochastic factors such as rainfall intensity or the occurrence of wildfires.

The 'discovery' of so-called 'range lands' has also led to a reassessment of the role and meaning of human activities in these same contexts. Long-term human activities have turned out to be not an extraneous or disturbing element of ecological systems, but an integral part of their functioning. This also requires us to rethink the notion of habitat, which should be understood not so much as the set of environmental conditions in which certain species of animals or plants live, but as the co-product of anthropic and non-anthropic activities that interact in maintaining dynamic balances functional to the preservation of an ecosystem. Basically, it means that there is no sort of initial stage to return to, no zero point or a moment in human history when the local environment was unaltered. At the stage when colonial occupation began, the local context was already characterized by a series of historical configurations that had helped to redefine the internal relationships within the local biosphere. It also means that pastoralism, through the walking of cattle, can contribute to the regeneration of pastures through the spreading of animal droppings or by contributing to the dispersal of seeds, and to their preservation through, for example, the constant removal of undergrowth, which prevents the development of fires, or, vice versa, through the practice of controlled burning. All this, however, depends on how these activities are carried out and their interactions with the other variables that contribute to defining them.

In the case of Senegal, the drafting of a pastoral code that includes the recognition and protection of land rights related to this activity has been on the agenda since 1975, but has yet to be implemented, unlike in other countries in the area. In 2000, for example, Mauritania adopted a pioneering code for protecting the freedom of pastoral mobility and giving this activity priority rights over grazing areas. Although they have the merit of having anticipated the lawmaking process since the 1990s, Niger and Guinea, and more recently Mali (2001) and Burkina Faso (2002), have also adopted pastoral laws and codes, but they struggle to implement them (Bonnet and Hérault, 2011). In the 1990s, the survival of pastoral systems during the great droughts of 1973 and 1984, and their ability to reconstitute themselves afterwards, had contributed to the revaluation of this activity even by key policy makers and development planners. Yet, while in some cases they devote important chapters to the issue of mobility, including cross-border mobility, the regulations in question tend to pander to a top-down bureaucratic approach, pursuing the technocratic-developmentalist vision that has historically characterized the state's approach to the pastoral question.

Today, pastoralism is finally beginning to receive attention as a practice capable of contributing to the development of territories deeply marked by the effects of climate change. Recently, Sahelian pastoral systems have also received attention for their contribution to the political stability of the territories involved. In 2013, the Djamena Declaration underlined their importance in terms of governance and territorial cohesion. An important stance considering that, in addition to climate challenges, pastoral systems also face other types of uncertainties related to geopolitical events and the internal politics of individual states. However, this increased attention has not always and necessarily translated into consequent territorial and agricultural policies; on the contrary, there has been a tendency towards the affirmation of a developmentalist approach that, precisely by focusing on the resilience potential of pastoral systems, has ended up abandoning them even more to themselves, increasing their precariousness (Duteurtre and Faye, 2009).

In 2013, there was a new revival of the proposal for a pastoral code in Senegal, but this has not yet resulted in a final text. Pastoralism still finds itself fragmented in a set of texts that directly and indirectly legislate in this area. The National Land Law, which has regulated land ownership in Senegal since independence, although innovative in some respects, included grazing land in the *zones de terroirs* for agricultural use. The management of pastures found itself divided and harnessed in a new territoriality compared to traditional management, under new authorities and bureaucratic rules whose rationality and rigidity clashed with the flexibility and management typical of these spaces. A first legal definition of pasture lands can be found in Decree No. 268 passed in 1980, regulating pastoral transit routes and the use of pastures and pastoral water points. Pastoral areas are defined as residual areas and understood as 'free spaces used or likely to be used for animal feeding',[20] weakening their preservation possibilities in the face of agricultural and urban advance. The precariousness of Senegal's pastoral land system is reflected in the agricultural and development policies dedicated to the sector.

Despite the progress that has been made in understanding the contribution of pastoralism to the nation's socio-economic well-being, Senegalese politicians tend to repeat old stigmatizations. The result is a kind of political schizophrenia that persists in affirming one principle in one reform and advocating the exact opposite in the next. In 2003, the Senegalese law on agricultural and forestry policy (Loi d'orientation agricole et sylvo-pastorale) finally recognized pastoralism as a form of valorization of rural space. The following year, the text of the New sectoral initiative for livestock development (Nouvelle Initiative sectorielle pour le développement de l'élevage) began by proclaiming the end of pastoralism as a political objective, specifying that: 'The image of starving and debilitated cattle wandering in search of hypothetical pastures and water points must disappear forever from the Senegalese agricultural landscape.' The same images of 'contemplative', 'anarchic and irrational' cattle breeding also reappear in the text.[21]

The decrease in the living space of pastoralism cannot only be countered by the almost paternalistic exhortation to the farmer to adapt to the times and decide to change (or modernize), but requires suitable accompanying measures. These cannot only be of a technical nature or devoted to learning other production methods but require commitments of a purely economic nature. Decreasing the space has a cost, which is calculated in more fodder to buy, more vaccines due to the degradation of the animal's life, the provision of adequate water resources and suitable storage facilities. However, the new development policies, as well as for small-scale agriculture, in fact do not even seem to have the interest in convincing pastoral systems to change their logic, integrating them into commercial chains. Rather, the aim is to exclude them from the political horizon, creating alongside them a parallel, dynamic and avant-garde supply chain, highly mechanized and based on selected cattle breeds.

2

Africa as the Granary of the World? Land, Extractivism and Global Food Security

The land rush and the new extractivism

Part of global public opinion probably started to take an interest in the existence of an agricultural land acquisition race in 2008, when the *Financial Times* (Jung-A et al, 2008) broke the news of ongoing negotiations between the South Korean company Daewoo Logistic and the government of Madagascar for the free grant of 1,300,000 hectares, equivalent to about half of the entire arable land of the African country, spread over several regions. According to the agreements, the land was to be used for the cultivation of maize and African oil palm. The company planned to export the harvests by placing them on the global market, but also intended to use them for the Korean market in the event of a new food crisis, similar to the global one that was underway at the time.

'Food can be a weapon in this world', said one of Daewoo's managers in an interview to explain the company's strategy, pointing out that the land involved was in an area that was 'totally undeveloped land which has been left untouched. And we will provide jobs for them by farming it, which is good for Madagascar' (Jung-A et al, 2008). The news of the agreements provoked protests and street riots in the country, leading to the dismissal of the incumbent president and forcing the new government to renege on the investment. It was also for this reason that the episode immediately found an echo in the media and contributed to opening an international debate, especially since, at the same time as that of the South Korean company, other similar operations were taking place, although with less media coverage, in very different places, from Europe to Brazil.

Those negotiations can be seen as an indication of a radical change that has taken place in the global economic system over the last few decades, directly involving the role of agrarian property, the structure of the production system and the distribution chain of agricultural products and is now exacerbating the clash between radically opposed ways of conceiving and inhabiting the land, and of organizing communal life and its reproduction.

Already since the oil crisis of the early 1970s, the agri-food industry had begun to withdraw from direct production to concentrate on activities that were considered more remunerative in the value chain, such as processing and distribution, where profit margins are higher. Primary production was in fact considered economically less attractive and inherently riskier, for economic reasons (related to the uncertainty of land yields due to random weather conditions, the presence of pests, and so on) and political reasons (risk of conflict, political instability, and so on). This picture was reversed in the early 2000s when the upward trend in commodity prices also increased the risks for suppliers and providers, not only for agricultural producers. The price crisis, the growing climatic instability and the gradual decrease in the yields of agricultural land, strained by the intensive production methods of industrial agriculture, seemed at that point to have convinced many multinationals in the sector of the need to regain direct control over primary production.

For instance, in July 2014, the Ferrero group bought the Turkish group Oltan, world leader in the production and marketing of hazelnuts. As explained by the company, the purchase was decided following a surge in the price of hazelnuts due to an unseasonal snowfall that had ruined the harvests, causing a loss of around 70 per cent (Scagliarini, 2014). The Bonduelle group, one of the world's leading distributors of canned vegetables, started a campaign to acquire farmland back in 2004. In 2014, it came to own some 11,000 hectares in Russia, where it grows maize and peas, as well as 1,500 hectares in Ukraine (Machart, 2014). At the same time, the Tereos cooperative sugar group managed 90,000 hectares of land for sugar cane production: 75,000 in Brazil and 15,000 in Mozambique (Machart, 2014).

Entering into direct production is a choice that spares companies the need to purchase raw materials on the market and at the same time allows them to invest in an asset, arable land, whose value can become increasingly high, and which also includes the value of the water resources it contains. The global distribution of land and crop ownership, on the other hand, represents an insurance mechanism against climatic variations that might affect a given area and ruin harvests, as well as a guarantee of steady product supply. These strategies do not follow directly from the logic of agricultural production, but are rather an attempt to influence markets by creating vertically integrated closed chains of production and distribution (Smaller and Mann, 2009). Such structures make it possible to exert full control from the place of production to the consumer. In this sense, the key action is no longer to link local production to a global market or obtain a competitive advantage in the large-scale production of local crops for their marketing, but to secure the stable supply of raw materials.

Alongside these mechanisms, others have set in. First of all, the possibility of using agricultural products to produce energy has attracted the attention of many new investors and prompted many agribusinesses to rethink their supply chain strategies. At the same time, land and agricultural production have also become 'secure' assets in an investment portfolio for an increasingly instable financial sector, traditionally unrelated to primary production (Fairbairn, 2014). Recent land investments are also motivated by the possibilities offered by so-called climate markets, such as stock carbon markets, as well as investments in global warming mitigation, renewable energy and environmental tourism (Fairhead et al, 2012). These trends are particularly present in the African context where various forms of investment and different trajectories of land exploitation often coexist.

Accumulation by exclusion

Although driven by a particular combination of economic and ecological crises, recent investments merely reflect the trend that economic development has followed in many countries in the 'global South' over the past 30 years. Indeed, the extractivist model that many postcolonial states have implemented since the late 1980s does not seem to have been challenged. Moreover, and in relation to this, the neoliberal paradigm of 'food security' is reinforcing the ways in which capitalism has historically operated in Africa, highlighting the strongly colonial stance of the contemporary global economic regime. The attempt to protect and secure existing patterns of accumulation thus goes hand in hand with the need to preserve the structures of 'global capitalist modernity' (Büscher, 2012) encapsulated in the idea of the inexhaustibility of 'the frontier' and its resources, depicting Africa as an untapped continent and its inhabitants as subjects to be modernized.

Extractivism is a notion that has become established in the Latin American academic and civil society context to denounce the progressive tendency of the continent's economies to focus on the intensive exploitation of a single resource, be it gold or soya. The term became popular towards the end of the 2000s in conjunction with the reaffirmation of a productivist vision of development supported by an extractive export model and implemented by several national governments, including the newly-elected progressive left and centre-left governments (Acosta, 2013: Svampa, 2019), and in contrast to earlier attempts to promote national industrialization, undertaken since the 1960s with the aim of ending dependence on extra-continental imports. Initially limited to the resumption of the large-scale mining industry on the continent, the notion of extractivism was also extended to large-scale monocultures in order to emphasize the similarities, in terms of wealth extraction, redistribution of value and environmental impacts, between these two sectors. Indeed, the extractivist model, based on mining and oil deposits, also applies to industrial agriculture. That is, it implies a form of intensive-extensive exploitation of the land, carried out for purposes external to the territory itself and its local usages, and that occurs according to logic and interests that cannot be determined by the societies and communities inhabiting it.

Most critical analyses define extractivism as a high-risk economy that, on the one hand, puts territories in competition on a global scale and subjects them to the performance of financial markets, while, on the other hand, it carries out unsustainable activities that produce irreversible effects (Gudynas et al, 2009). Because of their high environmental impact, extractive practices leave devastated and often irretrievable territories behind, where previously existing activities, particularly local agricultural ones, are lost forever. The term also indicates an advanced phase of capitalism, which takes on increasingly deadly and destructive aspects in the course of its development, proving less and less able to guarantee the promise of a general increase in well-being and improvement in the living conditions of the population.

All this is partly reminiscent of the description of colonial economy and is strongly in line with the logic that underpinned it. As a matter of fact, the intensive exploitation of land undermines the possibility of developing parallel economic activities and implies the application of sacrificial logic, which serves to establish which territories are to be intensively and irreversibly exploited and which sections of the population are to be endangered, forced to migrate, or assigned to low-skilled, poorly paid and high-risk jobs. It follows that most of these practices stand in stark contradiction to democratic land management (Zibechi, 2020; Zibechi and Machado, 2023).

The current conjuncture that holds together extractivism, agro-industry and resource hoarding is also deeply rooted in the developmentalist approach as it has emerged in the context of the post-Second World War global geopolitical reorganization. In postcolonial states, development has historically formed the basis of what we can call the 'citizenship pact' between the state and the people. Until recently, the 'developmental state' (an expression that has long been debated[1]) was the bearer of a modernization project (Scott, 1998) aimed at the creation of a citizen-worker, for whom access to political rights went hand in hand with their inclusion in the national economy. A path that was also to entail the progressive proletarization of the population. In this sense, the 'developmentalist state' can be understood as the postcolonial version of the welfare state (Mezzadra and Neilson, 2014): it represents the way in which the state has become the guarantor of certain aspects of social life, promoting the well-being of the population through the development of the economy.

In his analysis of power in Western societies, Foucault (2008) pointed out how it is precisely this role of the state that lays the basis for its governmentalization, whereby power is exercised through the government of subjects and of their relations with the environment. In the context of neoliberal modernity, this mode of government also envisages the adaptation of the state's devices to the economic logic of the market. Yet, if, as the French philosopher explains, the biopolitics of the European state unfolds through the enhancement and manipulation of productive life, this also implies to discard unproductive lives through violent processes of hierarchization. It is above all Achille Mbembe, with his idea of necropolitics (Mbembe, 2003), who has developed the idea of people who are *disposable*, defining it as 'the generalized instrumentalization of human existence and the material destruction of human bodies and populations' based on a civilizing logic that binds together modernity and capitalism, state and development. Necropolitics thus reveals the very colonial nature of sovereignty itself, as it emerges in the modern context, together with the idea of race and progress. Today, reference to the idea of necropolitics is often found in analyses that highlight the widening of marginality and social exclusion on a global scale promoted by economic development and the market's inability to generate processes of inclusion extended to the entire social sphere.

The growing marginalization turned out to be a common dynamic in the context of land investments following the 2007–2008 crisis. As explained by Saskia Sassen (2010), it follows a core tendency in current economic development processes such that 'resources and land matter, but people and their work don't'. In order to understand the meaning of this statement, it is worth bearing in mind how recent investments took place in the framework of a general and long-standing economic downturn, rooted in the crisis of Fordism, which resulted in the consequent financialization of the productive systems (Fumagalli and Mezzadra, 2010). Consistent with the capitalist way of managing the crisis, the financialization of the economy has also represented an attempt to reorganize the accumulation processes towards a perspective that is less and less guided by a productivist logic and more and more index-linked to forms of 'direct' value capture from the sphere of social and ecological reproduction (Boyd et al, 2011; Benegiamo, 2021).

Indeed, as feminist and postcolonial debates have shown, in order to grasp the logic of accumulation one should consider the structural relationship that binds together 'inclusion through exploitation' and 'exclusion through dispossession', that is, processes often described as disjointed. In this sense, both the continuous reproduction of the so-called primitive accumulation and the subordination of social and ecological reproduction are functional elements of capital valorization. Although formally external to the commodity production process, they stand for its own condition of possibilities. In relation to this, the recent wave of agricultural investments in most of the African continent thus show the attempts of the global food regime (McMichael, 2009) to integrate the multiple socio-economic, reproductive, and environmental crises into a broader accumulation revival strategy. They also imply a further phase of the globalization process (Sassen, 2013), in which food, energy and climate have become an increasingly integrated global nexus connecting territories through their forcible integration into financial markets and logics.

A 'competitive' agriculture

Today, agrarian extractivism thus seems to loom large as the main feature of African progress, at least in the ideas of the world's development institutions and the so-called global governance, which are among the continent's biggest policy funders. In its *Development Report* of 2008 (World Bank, 2007a), a peak year for large-scale agricultural investments, the World Bank classified the world's economies on a time axis, dividing them into 'agriculture-based countries', 'transforming countries' and 'urbanized countries'. The first category included sub-Saharan African countries, the second included much of South-East Asia, the Middle East and North Africa, and the third included parts of Latin America, Europe and Central Asia. The classification was based on the weight of agriculture in national growth, that is, the percentage of gross domestic product employed, combined with the rural poverty index. From this subdivision, and despite its backwardness index in a global economy, Africa's agricultural specialization could, according to the World Bank, be the basis of a 'comparative advantage', provided the continent was able to exploit its (supposed) availability of land and cheap labour.

The thesis of comparative advantage has often been re-proposed in national economic development projects. However, what is new in the Bank's use of this concept in this context is that it is associated with the idea of an agriculture that is no longer understood as the driving force behind the industrialization to come, as the old economic paradigms said, but as a sector to be developed in its own right. This conclusion is clear in the title of the report: *Agriculture for Development*, which presents agriculture as a means for development, marking a distance from the only other publication the Bank had devoted to the sector in 1982, *Agriculture and Development* (World Bank, 1982). Here agriculture was analysed in terms of its potential contribution to general economic development and, as just mentioned, its role was to be a driver for subsequent industrial development. However, if one reads between the lines, the emphasis on the economic potential of Africa's agricultural specialization rather hints to a theory of 'comparative disadvantage', that of a continent coming last in the race for progress. In the Bank's own words:

> Agriculture-based economies have largely missed the expansion of labor-intensive manufacturing that spurred development in Asia in the 1980s. There is still debate on the likelihood that Africa will emerge as a significant exporter of manufactured goods. But, based on current and emerging comparative advantage, a diverse portfolio of processed and unprocessed primary-based exports (including services such as tourism) will remain the main option for generating foreign exchange in the medium term. (World Bank, 2007a, p 34)

In addition to the idea that the development of commercial agriculture is necessary to attract foreign capital and essentially have the foreign currency required to make purchases on international markets as well as pay back debts previously incurred with development banks, the willingness to invest in land is also supported by the idea that agribusiness (and foreign investors) have more expertise than local agricultural systems when it comes to pursuing the goal of food security. Although this assertion conveys a long-standing assumption, it should be noted that this approach, in turn, strays from previous development paradigms, according to which, while remaining consistent with a developmentalist and productivist approach, it was the productive capacities of local farming systems that needed to be promoted, therefore assuming that the latter were both the object (and the subject) of development.

Rather, current development policies aim at a transformation of the agricultural model – the African one in particular, centred on small-scale family-based production into a commercial form of agriculture, more integrated into global markets, in terms of both agricultural inputs and outputs. On this basis, the World Bank also hopes for an increase in rural mobility and a decrease in the population involved in agricultural production.

Food security, a market paradigm

The signal that the world was heading for a new global food crisis came at the beginning of 2007, when a sudden surge in the prices of primary agricultural commodities (the so-called *soft commodities*) destabilized the agri-food trading markets. In the space of a year, between February 2007 and March 2008, the Food and Agriculture Organization (FAO) Food Price Index,[2] which measures the price trends of some of the most important food commodities, recorded an overall increase of 71 per cent.[3] In that period, the price of wheat rose by 80 per cent, maize by 90 per cent, soya oil by 199 per cent and coffee by 167 per cent.[4] Compared to the average price in 2002, the overall increase was as high as 130 per cent (Mitchell, 2008).

Rising costs have had repercussions throughout the agri-food chain, and the impact has been considerable for processors and distributors as well as consumers. The 'food crisis', as it was quickly dubbed, was felt the most in countries with low per capita income levels where, according to FAO estimates, 40 million people had become undernourished, in addition to the 923 million already existing in 2007 (FAO, 2008a). The situation got even worse in 2008–2009 with the further deepening of the economic-financial crisis generated by the collapse of the global financial system, also preceded by a new peak in oil prices in 2006. The problem of access to energy resources added to the problem of the high cost of living and, in turn, contributed to keeping food costs high, especially given agriculture's heavy dependence on the oil market (both for what concerns transport and mechanization and the massive use of crude oil derivatives in chemical fertilizers).

The protests were not long in coming. They spread in many countries, including in Europe, and took on drastic proportions where the crisis had struck the hardest. Dubbed 'food riots' by the world press (Bush, 2009), the protests took millions of people to the streets, particularly in the states with the lowest income populations. In Dakar, where the price of rice – a staple food for the Senegalese – rose by 35 per cent in a single day (Antil, 2010), an unauthorized demonstration organized by the Senegalese consumers' association was severely repressed. Similar protests broke out a few days later in many other African countries, including Nigeria, Cameroon, Ivory Coast, Mozambique, Mauritania and Burkina Faso.

However, it would be wrong to trace these demonstrations back to the issue of access to food and its cost alone. Fully embedded in their respective national political histories, they rather conveyed a radical demand for change rooted in social and systemic criticism. Seen from this perspective, the uprisings linked to the high cost of living made it clear that the development and liberalization policies implemented over the last 40 years had failed and questioned the capacity of markets to guarantee food security.[5] The latter is a notion that emerged as a regulating principle of food policies in the late 1970s and later asserted itself in the early 1990s, coinciding with the neoliberal turn in global economic policy (Maxwell, 1996).

History of a concept

By the mid-1970s, the food question had come to the forefront, not least as a result of socio-climatic events that had occurred in the four corners of the globe in the previous years (floods in the Indian continent, crop frost in the former USSR, famine in the Sahel), which led to a significant drop in cereal reserves and a rise in prices (Rondeau, 1975). In November 1974, the United Nations General Assembly, under the responsibility of the Economic and Social Council, convened the first World Food Conference in Rome. The assembly, attended by representatives from 123 countries, concluded with the Universal Declaration on the Eradication of Hunger and Malnutrition

(United Nations, 1975). The Committee on World Food Security (CFS) was also created, which would act under the aegis of the FAO as the body to review food policies and issue guidelines.

Contrary to the position that was to become predominant a few years later, at the time of its creation, the prevailing view in the CFS was that the role of agricultural production was central to meeting food needs. The reference was to the notion of food security as defined by the 1974 conference: the 'availability, at all times, of adequate world supply of basic foodstuffs … to sustain a steady expansion of food consumption … and to offset fluctuations in production and prices' (United Nations, 1975, p 14). As a result, the actions to be taken were aimed at increasing production and stabilizing the world cereal market (CFS, 2012).

In the following years, however, the persistence of situations of chronic malnutrition urged the international institutions to change the definition of food security, recalibrating it on the problem of access to resources and no longer on the sole issue of production. Thus, in 1983, following a further food crisis, the FAO, with the approval of the CFS, redefined food security as the ability to ensure physical and economic access to necessary food for everyone at all times (FAO, 1983). Many definitions appeared later, but the one reformulated in 1996 by the FAO at the Second World Food Summit eventually became the reference for many national policies and planned interventions by international institutions. The latter definition, in turn, referred to that provided by the World Bank, in a report entitled *Poverty and Hunger*, which described food security as the act of 'ensuring that all people at all times have both physical and economic access to the basic food that they need … for an active, healthy life' (World Bank, 1986, p 1). In the 1996 version, food security was thus understood as the condition that 'exists when all people, at all times, have physical and economic access to sufficient, safe and nutritious food to meet their dietary needs and food preferences for an active and healthy life' (FAO, 1996).

Thus, the centrality of access to resources, established in the 1980s, was reconfirmed as a key dimension in ensuring food security, complemented by nutritional and health parameters adapted to different contexts. Access was also understood as physical, and took into account the necessary infrastructure, such as roads and storage centres, through which food is distributed, stored and bought. Moreover, access was not only understood in terms of the satisfaction of basic needs, but also of personal preferences and inclinations, and included choice and thus differentiation of supply.

The shift in focus from a strategy of production to one of access defined in these terms would, according to the approach of leading international bodies, result in greater reliability in the market as the guarantor of food security. The thesis was that the market, as an institution capable of and suitable for matching supply and demand, was able to allocate food more efficiently through distribution and trade networks. Food security therefore depended on the progressive integration of trade between countries with a production surplus and countries with a deficit, supplemented by food aid flows and the economic capacity of individuals to obtain these primary goods, finally made accessible on the market.

Peasant crises and new ecological movements

The issue of food security has become increasingly important with the transformations of the global distribution system and the penetration of finance into agriculture and the global food system. Reconsidered in light of these changes, the idea of food security, which spread in the early 1990s, was an alternative to, and in contrast with, the dirigiste policies implemented by postcolonial socialist governments to achieve food self-sufficiency.[6] In the 1960s and 1970s, in fact, most recently independent governments in Africa had proposed agricultural policies centred on the promotion of and reliance on local small-scale farming systems in order to achieve self-sufficiency in meeting national needs. The idea of security directly opposes that of self-sufficiency, suggesting that the state should rather be concerned with monitoring the proper functioning of internal storage and transport networks and keeping the trade balance under control to be able to subsidize imports.

The shift to a neoliberal interpretation of the hunger problem has thus acquired specific political significance and affected the investment choices of many governments in the global South. Accordingly, in many postcolonial economies, reprimarization, or extractivism, has grown in the last decades, in correspondence to a tendency towards de-industralization (Muradian and Martínez-Alier, 2001; Herreros and Lima, 2011) and has coincided, on a global level, with the expansion of commodity frontiers (Moore, 2000) into territories and natures not yet commodified. There have been two main drivers of this shift. Firstly, the liberalization of key sectors related to energy production and the extraction of raw materials, as a direct effect of the implementation of the structural adjustment plans imposed by the World Bank and the International Monetary Fund during the 1980s and 1990s. Added to this was the progressive agricultural mono-specialization aimed at exports, whose logic differed from that of the agricultural monocultures implemented since the 1950s, as they were placed in the new context of the neoliberalization of the global agricultural market, the consequent reorganization of production and the crisis of small-scale agriculture at a national level.

The liberalization of agricultural markets has ended up eroding the farmers' bargaining power in the context of a global restructuring of power relations in marketing chains (Patel, 2007; Van der Ploeg, 2012). It has also decreased the share of value accruing to producers and undermined the standard of living of smallholder farmers. At the same time, the expansion of a global agricultural market controlled by large financialized corporations has led to the rapid shift of production to those areas able to bear lower wages, promoting social differentiation both locally and inter-regionally. It has also made the agro-industrial model of large estates, which are able to absorb price volatility through technical innovations and expansion of production scales, more economically viable (Baglioni and Gibbon, 2013).

The social transformations induced by neoliberal processes influenced the political proposals put forward by the social movements in rural areas in those years and led to an increase in ecological claims and environmental conflicts. Rural populations, particularly in the 'global South', often found themselves fighting not only against new processes of land and seed privatization (Shiva, 2016), but also against environmental degradation and in defence of ecosystems. They mobilized in conflicts that put environmental protection and the defence of local production systems on the same level, which were increasingly being threatened by the expansion of extractive industries and mega-projects (mines, dams, plantations, energy and transport infrastructures). Political ecology, as a field of scholarly debate, has paid enormous attention to these struggles, which have been seen as a form of 'ecologism of the poor' and 'conflicts over ecological distribution', part of a global movement for environmental justice (Martínez-Alier, 2002).

In many cases, the expansion of ecological struggles has also entailed the redefinition from an 'identity' point of view of the social claims made by rural movements as well as the rethinking of the notion of autonomy (Li, 2000; Geschiere, 2009; Fulmer, 2011). In Latin America, for example, the idea of autochthony and mechanisms such as those of the 'community consultation' have become pivotal tools for domestic negotiations between the state and various social groups, particularly indigenous and native peoples, in deciding territorial policies and against the intensive exploitation of the territory and its resources (Flores and Guerriero, 2016) The significant cultural legacy of these experiences, which are still underway, has made it possible to develop alternative ideas and concepts that are rethinking human well-being beyond growth-based development (Kothari et al, 2019).

As far as agricultural production is concerned, the notion of food sovereignty promoted by the international movement Via Campesina since the early 1990s is of particular relevance, precisely in opposition to the concept of food security that emerged in the same period (Patel, 2009). Defined by Via Campesina as 'the peoples', Countries' or State Unions' RIGHT to define their agricultural and food policy, without any dumping vis-à-vis third countries',[7] the idea of food sovereignty was initially conceived as a tool to allow states to claim their autonomy in defining agricultural and food policies, thus countering the obligations imposed by liberalization policies decided at an international level. In recent years, the concept of food sovereignty has increasingly become the symbol of a global struggle taken up by 'a small farmer and peasant movement' to denounce the failure of agricultural liberalization policies centred on the paradigm of food security and to affirm the central role of small-scale and family agricultural production in the realization of the human right to food.

The emergence of the food security paradigm, and its neoliberal redefinition in the 1990s, must therefore be traced back to a geopolitical context characterized, in its recent history, also by the peak and subsequent decline of 'Third World' national liberation movements, to which new claims marked by a strong ecological stance and the defence of the territory have followed. The idea of food security must also be understood in relation to the gradual establishment of a new structure of the world economic system that took shape in 1994 with the creation of the World Trade Organization, after seven and a half years of extremely long negotiations involving 123 countries (the so-called Uruguay Round, which lasted from 1986 to 1994), during which the main bone of contention was precisely the regulation of agricultural markets.

The idea of a 'new international economic order' to deal with the problem of access to food was already present in the *Universal Declaration on the Eradication of Hunger and Malnutrition*, which repeated the concept twice in its introduction. However, it is important to emphasize that, far more than the liberalization of trade sanctioned by the World Trade Organization, what has most influenced the evolution of the agri-food system and the set of economic policies on a global level has been the progressive liberalization of the financial markets undertaken by the neoliberal governments of Reagan and Thatcher, as well as by Mitterrand's government in France.[8] In fact, as already mentioned, freedom of movement for capital has allowed the internationalization and growth of big multinationals involved in the distribution and processing of foodstuffs, which have thus succeeded in imposing a monopolistic 'bottleneck' management of the food supply system (Patel, 2007), with few companies at the top, with the power of centralizing and conditioning multiple local producers at a global level.

From food security to global food security

The idea of food security outlined so far has remained at the heart of the institutional rhetoric adopted in response to the 2008 food crisis, just as the definition approved in 1996 was re-proposed by the FAO at the conclusion of the World Summit on Food Security held in Rome in 2009. On that occasion, the addition of the notion of social access to that of physical and economic access expressed the partial integration in the text of the criticism made by civil society organizations (Patel, 2009). Yet, with respect to an essentially unchanged definition, the factors identified as the basis of food insecurity and the policy solutions proposed today and adopted in the immediate post-crisis period differ from the previous ones on at least six points:

1. the emergence of the food issue as a global security problem that, as such, requires political regulation to be implemented through the strengthening of global governance mechanisms;
2. the integration of the food issue with those of the environmental-climatic crisis and the economic crisis;
3. the identification of new geopolitical scenarios, drawn on the basis of the new patterns and geographies of supply and demand;
4. the revived emphasis on the increase in agricultural production and the role of national policies in promoting this increase;
5. a new vision of the role of private actors as the main sponsors and promoters of development programmes, which ties in with the growing role of capitalist philanthropic foundations, including those belonging to multinationals in the sector; and, finally,
6. the central role of Africa (or rather, of its lands) as an active part of the solution.

A global solution

The letter that the Federal Chancellor of Germany, Angela Merkel, addressed to G8 members in July 2008 (DW, 2008) clarifies the implications of redefining the idea of security from a global perspective. It states that, with the spread of revolts in several countries, undernourishment is no longer perceived as a problem affecting individual states but must now be considered as a source of global instability. Therefore, hunger has turned into a potential threat to global security and implies intervention and regulation on an equal scale. The governments' awareness of their dependence on the fluctuations of increasingly unstable commodity markets has helped to put the issue of food availability back on the global political agenda. However, this has not led to a revision of the neoliberal logic: what is required is a surplus of political action as well as global coordination to enable the agribusiness industrial system to adapt and cope with the food crisis, and with the cheap food crisis, as well as imagine its reorganization in line with the modernist, technical paradigm of economic growth.

There were two main responses to the food crisis. The first emergency response called for increased funding and networks to send food aid where needed. In a long-term perspective, the second one proposed the need for both a political and a coordinated effort to promote investments to boost agricultural production. In tune with this approach, the FAO itself declared, at the outcome of the 2008 conference on the food crisis, that 'we cannot rely on the balancing virtues of market forces to overcome the food crisis and hold out the prospect of real food security. We can and must recognize the need for policies and interventions that are framed and delivered within the United Nations system' (FAO, 2008b, pp 9–10). A statement that we could take as a symbol of the transition from the era of *food security* to that of *global food security*, which maintains the notion of security, but projects it on a global scale.

This reflects the stance of the main development and global governance institutions, such as the World Bank, the World Trade Organization, the Organization for Economic Co-operation and Development, and the G8 and G20 summits. The latter have integrated food security into their political agenda and envisaged financial support on a permanent basis for the first time, in the wake of the Aquila Food Security Initiative, which was launched at the 2009 G8 Summit, held in L'Aquila, Italy, from 8 to 10 July, and later confirmed at the G20 Summit in Pittsburgh, USA (Margulis, 2012). Despite a few differences, all these initiatives confirm a common framework within which the global food problem is being considered and national and regional agricultural development policies are being rewritten.

The existence of a shared vision is also confirmed by the close connection between the various initiatives that support one another and mutually interact: the Aquila Food Security Initiative supports the 'Global Agriculture and Food Security Programme' promoted by the World Bank, which is based on the 'Five Principles for Sustainable Global Food Security' adopted in November 2009 by the World Summit on Food Security held in Rome, also built on the Aquila Food Security Initiative approach. All these initiatives have also established greater coordination and participation of private sector actors. Representatives of major food, bio and agro-technology as well as logistics industries participated in a parallel event held in the framework of the preparations for the World Summit on Food Security. On the other hand, in 2009, the industry partners of the World Economic Forum launched the New Vision for Agriculture initiative, with the aim of organizing public–private partnerships in Asia and Africa with the support of the International Fund for Agricultural Development, which, together with the World Bank, is the main financing agency of the United Nations.

The effectiveness of the initiatives implemented cannot easily be quantified. However, as the numerous rural grassroots movements denounce, it remains highly unlikely that the choices and actors who actively contributed to the creation of the problem can possibly be part of its solution. What is certain, however, is that while the majority of the world's population suffered food shortages as a result of the market turmoil that erupted in 2008, the top 20 agribusiness multinationals recorded profits of almost 250 billion dollars (191 billion euros; data based on the period 2003–2012), which placed them ahead of the automotive giants (179 billion euros for Toyota, Volkswagen, BMW,

Renault and Ford over the same period) and investment banks (171 billion euros for JPMorgan, Goldman Sachs and Morgan Stanley) (Damgé, 2013).

Feeding ten billion people?

The recurrence of the problem of agricultural land productivity has, in turn, characterized this new phase of development, on two accounts: the progressive decrease in agricultural yields and the increase in global demand for food. While the first factor is indeed a demonstrable fact and the result of the expansion of industrial monocultures,[9] which require intensive methods of soil exploitation, the second aspect is much more controversial. Consider, for example, the often quoted need to double agricultural production between now and 2050 (United Nations, 2009). This concept has sparked many national debates, but it is not clear on what analyses or calculations this figure was based.

This topic was analysed in detail by the Environment, Food and Rural Affairs Committee – a British governmental body appointed by the House of Commons[10] – which asked the government to give answers in this regard (UK, 2010) and by the Soil Association, a non-governmental organization concerned about the relevance that this figure had acquired in the debate underway in English-speaking countries. What they found out, however, is that no quantitative analysis supporting this objective ever existed either in FAO reports or in any documents used by the British government (Soil Association, 2010). The only figures found in FAO reports published in 2006 mention a 70 (and not a 100) per cent increase by 2050, and only in certain production areas, that is, the grain and meat sectors, mainly because the purpose of grains is feeding cattle, a basic product of the latter (FAO, 2009b)

In order to better understand the problem of increasing yields and food supply, we should therefore mention another aspect, centred on the role of so-called empty, under-exploited or potentially arable land. This notion has a colonial origin (Li, 2014[b]) and has been associated with that of marginal lands for a few years now. The former refers to the idea of land that is not in use, or whose agricultural potential remains unexplored and inadequately exploited. Marginality, on the other hand, is understood as the consequence of the poverty of the occupants who, judged to be lacking in means, are unable to respond autonomously to the new demands for growth and intensification of exploitation of their territories, so that external intervention is required to replace or integrate local farming systems into global value chains. Within this discourse, sub-Saharan Africa has become a strategic space for the new development strategies.

In its report *Awakening Africa's Sleeping Giants* published in 2009 (Morris et al, 2009), the World Bank described the Guinean savannah as one of the largest under-utilized reserves of agricultural land in the world, insisting that distinctly underexplored agricultural potentials lie hidden throughout Africa, including the semi-desert areas. The African continent comes to be described as an area with an abundance of arable land or potential arable land that can ensure the development of agro-industry, host food production capable of responding to the global food security problem, and contribute to the transition to renewable sources through the production of biomass for agrofuels. Indeed, agricultural development is not limited to food objectives but could also be the key to producing renewable energy, mitigating the climate, contributing to environmental conservation, or doing all three things at the same time. The advent of a new *climate-smart agriculture* is advocated, where the idea of the future of agriculture imagines improved, drought-tolerant and higher-yielding seed crops which will also serve as a means with which to combat climate change, increase the resilience of territories and reduce carbon emissions.

Private actors have given voice to this new dogma. Philippa Purser, then Managing Director at Cargill Australia, stated that Africa, with its abundance of land, was to be a 'piece of the answer' (Wagstaff, 2014) to the current resource crisis. Cargill, one of the top six agribusiness multinationals that together cover more than 70 per cent of the market,[11] is active on the continent today through its foundation, with a series of programmes ranging from credit facilities for the purchase of its products to partnerships with public and private laboratories for the genetic modification of native and non-native species. This approach is based on the implicit assumption that smallholder farmers do not need fairer access to water and land, or better infrastructures to sell and store their produce, which is one of the main problems faced by African farmers, but rather that they should go further into debt to access technologies whose capacity to increase yields and make family and small-scale farming more profitable has been challenged by a number of studies (see, for example, Patel, 2013). Basically, this is the old proposal to modernize peasant agriculture by transforming it into an agriculture based on the intensive use of agrochemicals and biotechnology so that it can be included in global trade chains. In practice, however, this approach has widened the social gap between those who could access development programmes and those who did not have the means to do so (for instance, peasants who do not own land or are unable to incur debt) and boosted the large-scale monocultures for which those products were designed and developed (Amanor, 2012).

Growth, economic revitalization, new opportunities for global capital, poverty reduction, protection of small-scale family farming, increasing food availability, energy transition, combating the climate crisis. All these prospects seem possible and achievable through agricultural development, provided that the radical transformation of African agriculture becomes an unavoidable goal, as Kofi Annan, former United Nations Secretary

General on a visit to Burkina Faso, explained well: 'We can feed ourselves in Burkina, in Africa, and even help the whole world to feed itself. We just need to transform agriculture' (Akinocho, 2014). This vision emphasized the need for 'privately-driven development', with a view to also stimulating the arrival of investors interested in promoting agro-industrial projects. Resorting to private intervention was mostly justified by the long-standing decline in development aids and the impact of the 2008 economic crisis on the ability of governments to incur debt and finance public and research programmes. As noted by Raj Patel (2013, p 43), this replaced previous approaches centred on the mechanism of public subsidies to farmers, and instead placed a strong emphasis on the 'the fungibility of land as a *sine qua non* of agricultural progress'.

3

Narratives and Failures of Green Development

Land-grabbing and development in postcolonial Senegal

In the years immediately after the global food crisis, the expression 'land-grabbing' became widely used in the media. While this term is important in defining a further stage of 'accumulation by dispossession' associated with land, particularly in Africa, it remains nonetheless vague with respect to the dynamics and processes that such dispossession entails and on which it is based.

In a very general way, and when used to refer to the land acquisitions of the early 2000s, this idea refers to the land concentration dynamics that have oriented post-crisis agricultural development since 2007–2008. Sustained by a precise political approach, the new development indications remain consistent with the idea that the industrial agricultural model – characterized by monoculture and intensive land exploitation, as well as by the increasing financialization of agricultural markets and a monopolistic organization of distribution chains on a global scale – is better suited to combine the promotion of local development, global food supply and climate change mitigation actions, in particular because of its greater capacity for investment and technological promotion as compared to peasant, local and small-scale agriculture. In this sense, it is a vision strongly revolving around a pro-growth technocratic approach, based on a neoliberal preference for free trade and the central role supposedly played by competition for the proper functioning of the market. A vision that, as we have seen, goes hand in hand with the rhetoric of an abundance of arable land and biodiversity that conveyed the (re)inclusion of sub-Saharan Africa in the global economic policy following the 2007–2008 crisis. Recent approaches to agricultural development thus end up reiterating a colonial-era conception of land availability. This hypothesis sees the 'global South' as the main 'frontier' of agro-extractivist development and indigenous subjectivities as enemies, threating the social organizations and the sense of cultural identity of many and indigenous populations.

In order to sustain these assumptions, ideological and material multi-layered narratives are required that act at both the temporal and geographical levels. At the turn of the millennium, three specific narratives played a central role in sustaining the land rush phenomena, concerning respectively the idea of modernization; the imperative of energy transition; and the emphasis on the capabilities offered by private investors, who were seen as 'enlightened' actors and promoters of development. Unlike the other two, the first narrative has a very long history behind it, whose origins can be traced back to the context of colonial economy. Since then, there have been numerous variations and adjustments. Today, the modernist rhetoric responds above all to the neoliberal approach towards individualization and self-empowerment, which has been accompanied by the dismantling of social protection and public support systems. The dismantling of welfare has gone hand in hand with the deregulation of environmental issues following distinct, though related, paths in the welfarist democracies of the Fordist state and in postcolonial and developmentalist contexts. Furthermore, the integration of the costs of social and environmental reproduction into the market has ended up shifting the burden onto the individual.

The history of agricultural development in Senegal reveals the inconsistencies of the modernist approach and its failed outcomes quite clearly. Focused on a contradictory dynamic that has organized the continuity between its colonial past and a reformist approach since the proclamation of independence (obtained on 20 August 1960[1]), the Senegalese agricultural policy has in fact remained consistent with the typical principle of colonial economy that organized the territory into regional extractive enclaves mostly created from scratch. While declaring the firm intention to reform colonial marketing circuits, the new governmental apparatuses were conditioned by the bureaucracy they had inherited, which they perpetuated through the nationalization of colonial trade structures.

The defence of the old surplus generating mechanisms, which was being transferred to the state apparatus, was also evident in the focus on the groundnut, the main colonial export commodity, and the progressive specialization in rice-growing in the Senegal River delta region. At the same time, when Senegal gained independence, the socialist vision of development, which the country was promoting together with other African states,[2] came to be understood as a radical project of social transformation aimed at national unification and oriented towards equality and social well-being. In particular, agricultural development must meet the nation's needs with a view to food self-sufficiency, which also implied a process of individual improvement and empowerment. Rural dwellers, who made up the vast majority of the Senegalese population at that time, were called upon to contribute equally, on the basis of their labour, to their well-being through participation in the national economy. An essential role was attributed to the agricultural cooperatives introduced by the former colonial power, which rapidly grew in number in the first decades of independence. In 1960, the year of independence, there were 812 farmer cooperatives in Senegal, and by the following year there were 1,200 of them (Minvielle and Lailler, 2005, p 35).

The contradictions of African socialism

Cooperatives were conceived as the main means to assimilate small-scale farmers into the nationalization process. Through them, the state could intervene in the rural environment, regulating and directing production. The government undertook to provide credit to the cooperatives through the Senegalese Development Bank, to distribute seeds and to buy crops at a guaranteed price. Development policies also included the establishment of public bodies to cover the main aspects of rural life, such as health or education.

In addition to the socialist vision, the cooperatives' policy could also rely on another type of support revolving around the Sufist way of life preached by the Islamic Mouride brotherhood, which identifies work – particularly in agriculture – as a high form of prayer and a mystical practice to access God (Copans, 1980). A vision that has its origins precisely in the agricultural work communities, still existing today, created in the second half of the 19th century by the confraternity's founder Aḥmed Muḥammad Ḥabīb Allāh, better known by the name of Amadu Bamba Mbacké, whose image is frequently seen on the walls of Senegalese homes. However, and despite declared intentions, the emphasis on increasing productivity – in turn based on a merely technical vertical approach, combined with the political-economic interests of the various elites and the difficulties inherited from the colonial period – ended up prevailing over the prospect of a holistic participation of individuals in rural development.

Moreover, the socialist approach of the time was not without its problems or contradictions, especially since it was itself rooted in a progressive vision of the economy and society that saw the process of modernization of the rural masses as the main way to realize the utopias of prosperity and equality. Compared to this, the idea of African socialism, of which the first president of independent Senegal Léopold Sédar Senghor was one of the greatest theoretical exponents, introduced a political theory of decolonization that, unlike European-style socialism, sidestepped the question of (class) conflict within society, proclaiming a national homogeneity embodied in the idea of African people (Senghor, 1971).

Justified also in the name of the continent's failed agro-industrial revolution and of a unity of the African people in the face of the colonization experience, this approach nevertheless ended up bringing about the ideological removal of the social differences that had come into being during the colonial period and were passed on to the new phase (Mamadou, 1996). Behind the 'rhetoric' of the African people and national development lay in fact the question of ethnic and class identities and their reconfiguration around the new axes of power (Mamadou, 1996). Ethnic alliances in particular, far from being overcome and recomposed through the category of citizenship, which ideally referred to an undifferentiated and non-characterized individual, were opportunistically, and manipulatively, reorganized within the crony bureaucracy of nascent African states (Bayart, 2006), a strategy that became central for the preservation of power up to the present day.

Instead, the centrality of the state as guarantor and advocate of national unity and promoter of economic development was retained from the 'established' socialist hypothesis. The result of all this was a process of nationalization of which the agrarian question, in its two components of land policy and agricultural policy, represented one of the highest expressions; however, it would in many ways prove incapable of coping with the contradictions inherent in the emerging postcolonial state. On the one hand, the nationalization of land sanctioned in 1964 by a pioneering law on common property (Le Roy, 1985) did not achieve the abolition of customary law, but on the other hand it facilitated the continuity and sedimentation of local powers, whose formation coincided with the colonial period (Faye, 2008). It was precisely the local powers that found themselves occupying prominent positions in the nascent institutions at the regional and provincial levels. Moreover, while public support and intervention in the sale prices of agricultural produce were the pillar of Senegalese agricultural policy and the main incentives for the expansion of food crops, everything was also conditional on the availability of liquidity in an economy mainly dependent on peanut exports.

This legume crop accounted for 80 to 85 per cent of exports during the early years of independence, placing the country as the fourth largest producer in the world (Minvielle and Lailler, 2005, p 24). Despite its importance, the groundnut economy rested on a fragile balance. At the time of independence, 80 per cent of exports were absorbed by Italy and France. The latter, in particular, based 60 per cent of its vegetable oil consumption on Senegalese groundnuts, which it imported at an agreed price. When France discontinued its most-favoured-nation treatment policy towards Senegal in 1967, the groundnut experienced its first crisis. The alignment with the world market caused the price to fall and Senegal to lose about 20 per cent of its export turnover (Minvielle and Lailler, 2005).

Groundnut exports also served to finance imports, particularly of rice, consumed both in the countryside and by an expanding urban population. At the time of independence, Senegal was among the most urbanized states in sub-Saharan Africa, and Dakar, already made important by its previous role as the capital of French West Africa, was a booming city. In order to meet food needs, the French colonial administration had opted to import rice processing waste from another colony, Indochina. This was the so-called 'broken rice', that is, fragments of rice grains, which is still the main staple of the national diet. Indeed, independent Senegal inherited and maintained the colonial dietary pattern, not least because reliance on imports had the function of keeping food prices low in the city.

Cereals such as rice and wheat proved to be better suited to urban consumption habits due to the shorter preparation time required compared to millet or other traditional crops. The early years of independence saw a sharp increase in imports of these cereals. The volume of imported wheat rose from 74 to 112 tonnes in ten years; today, Senegal alone absorbs more than 80 per cent of rice imports destined for West Africa (Minvielle and Lailler, 2005).

Structural adjustment policies and the 'farmers' malaise'

In independent Senegal, as in many other postcolonial states, it was the adoption of the Structural Adjustment Programmes[3] that marked a decisive turning point and put an end to the socialist experiences of the previous period. In 1980, with the debt crisis, Senegal was the first country in sub-Saharan Africa to sign a plan to revive the economy (the Plan de Redressement économique et financier [PREF; Economic and Financial Recovery Plan]) with the International Monetary Fund. The plan was to be carried out through a series of Structural Adjustment Programmes agreed with the World Bank. The adjustment policies were implemented gradually, not without resistance from the central government, which was reluctant to completely dismantle its structures (Ba, 2008).

The Structural Adjustment Programmes were first implemented through the adoption of a stabilization programme (Programme de stabilisation) in 1979 and an economic and financial recovery programme (Programme de redressement économique et financier), in force from 1981 to 1984, which opted for a decrease in public support for peanut production. Several food security plans were launched that set production targets. These targets were systematically disregarded, but the plans are still underway. But it is with the Nouvelle Politique Agricole [New Agricultural Policy], in force from 1985 to 1994, and the Programmes, Lettres et Déclarations de Politique Agricole [Programs, Letters, and Declarations of Agricultural Policy], active from 1995 to 2005, that the most influential changes took place and the reforms envisaged in the Structural Adjustment Plans were carried out.

The New Agricultural Policy, basically defined by the International Monetary Fund, envisaged the withdrawal of the state from certain agricultural sectors and the downsizing of the roles and functions of regional development companies (Sociétés Régionales de Développement), such as the Société nationale d'aménagement et d'exploitation des terres du delta du fleuve Sénégal [Senegal River Delta Land Development and Exploitation Company], as well as a reform of the cooperative system, which was to be transformed in accordance with a greater autonomy of grassroots organizations and local producer groups. A specific policy concerned the rice sector with the approval of the Programme d'Ajustement du Secteur Riz [Rice Sector Adjustment Programme] in 1994, financed by the US Development Agency, USAID, and followed by the closure of the Price Stabilization and Equalization Fund (Caisse de Stabilisation et Péréquation des Prix) in 1995.

In 1994, Senegal was also hit hard by the devaluation of its currency, the CFA franc, arbitrarily imposed by France, which opted for the default of the Senegalese currency.[4] The result was the inability of the national institutions to oppose the directives of the World Bank and the International Monetary Fund. Liberalization through price clearing and the promotion of private sector intervention in the agricultural market thus intensified. The peanut and cattle-farming sectors also met the same fate. With its accession to the World Trade Organization in 1995, Senegal finally had to reduce its customs tariffs and definitively divest itself of the role of the state as price regulator. It was hoped that private investment would increase in the country, but the only result was an increase in imports, facilitated by the new regulations. The liberalization policies brought local producers to their knees, who were unable to compete with the global market. In particular, without the subsidies, rice production in the Senegal Valley as a whole, including the delta, ceased to be economically viable for Senegalese farmers who, having to face up to the progressive liberalization of the supply chain, found themselves deprived of the means to cope with the low cost of imported rice (Koopman, 2012). This period of unease for small-scale farmers, called *le malaise paysan*, also coincided with the first great wave of migration and abandonment of the countryside.

The analysis of the new agricultural and land investments in the country cannot therefore be separated from the historical and social process described here, according to which the rural inhabitants' inability to take the place of the state in supporting agricultural growth and development is interpreted today, both by the government and by international donors, in terms of a personal and private failure, rather than being the effect of a failure to listen to the needs of the territory combined with the disinterest of institutions towards the local population. When, in the early 2000s, the then President Abdoulaye Wade[5] (head of the openly liberal Senegalese Democratic Party, which put an end for the first time to the 37-year rule of the socialist party founded by Léopold Sédar Senghor) issued a series of new measures and plans for agricultural development, the emphasis was on the need to attract the capital necessary to promote a conversion of the predominant agricultural system, characterized by small family structures, and move towards the creation of large-scale commercial farms capable of competing in regional and international markets.

This perspective brought about a substantial change in the Senegalese agricultural context, which, except for a limited number of enterprises, never had an agro-industrial sector based on large private commercial estates. According to data provided by the Food and Agriculture Organization, agro-industry in Senegal employed only 1 per cent of the working population on 5 per cent of the arable land, while 60 per cent of the national workforce was employed in family farming and cultivates plots with a per capita average of 0.25 hectares (FAO and IFC, 2016). Although the number of export companies engaged in the fruit and vegetable sector has grown since the 1970s, this trend remains limited to a few geographical areas and involves a small number of producers (Baglioni, 2015). It has also not led to a transformation of small-scale farming production methods, which mostly tend to remain disconnected from international supply chains in the organization of work (Baglioni, 2015).

With respect to this, the intention was to promote a 'two-speed' agrarian economy that, on the one hand, envisaged the modernization of those farmers who were able to sustain a transformation of the scales of production and, on the other hand, the creation of a parallel agribusiness sector through the promotion of measures that fostered entrepreneurship and support investments. This perspective also required a review of land access procedures and their 'simplification' to encourage investments (Benegiamo, 2020). The new agricultural policies, however, do not consider the numerous structural and material constraints that affect Senegalese farmers. Thus, while the latter essentially continue to suffer the negative consequences of three decades of liberalization, privatization and deflationary policies, large private investors benefit from political support as well as programmes and financial concessions cut out for them.

Italy seeks land in Senegal

The launch of the new policies to promote agro-industry in Senegal coincided with the end of the structural adjustment policies and the transition to a new set of programmes and aid designed mainly under the Heavily Indebted Poor Countries Initiative, promoted, once again, by the International Monetary Fund and the World Bank. Such policies were also carried out through a series of programmes presented by President A. Wade as a response to the 2007–2008 food and energy price crises that stirred up discontent and civil unrest, forcing the government to react. Many of these policies contained directions to allocate land in rural communities to private investors capable of establishing agrofuel cultivation and production projects. Among them, the Special Programme on Biofuels[6] – approved in 2007 as part of the Retour vers l'Agricolture (REVA; Return to Agriculture Plan),[7] financed by Spanish cooperation – envisaged the creation of integrated agricultural centres over a total of 321,000 hectares in its first implementation phase in the period 2007–2012. These were to be distributed among the 321 existing Senegalese rural communities with the objective of achieving a yearly production of 3,200 tonnes of Jatropha seeds. The expected output starting from 2012 was to be 1.19 billion litres of untreated oil. This prospect was presented as the solution to achieving energy independence and to creating a labour supply that could curb the rural exodus and give young migrants subject to European repatriation operations a reason not to leave their country.

In the early 2000s, that of agrofuels was one of the most pervasive narratives accompanying the first wave of agricultural investment. Oil seed plants such as Jatropha or soybean, maize or sunflower – so-called 'flexible' crops because they could ideally be destined for the food, energy or livestock markets, depending on the situation[8] – played a central role in the strategies of many of the investors who arrived in Africa between 2007 and 2012. According to the first report of the Land Matrix portal (Anseeuw et al, 2012), non-food and flexible crops accounted for 60 per cent of the investments for which reliable information was available. In 2013, the non-governmental organization GRAIN estimated that 45 per cent of the 17 million hectares dedicated to agrofuel production between 2002 and 2012 were in sub-Saharan Africa (GRAIN, 2013).

Interest in biomass production grew in the early 2000s, coinciding with the enactment of several national and supra-regional policies related to energy reconversion and leading to the consolidation of a global market by quadrupling the world supply of biomass in eight years (2000 to 2008) (IEA, 2009). The United States and the European Union have played an important role in promoting the demand for agrofuels and supporting their marketing, causing land-use change in several countries (Palmer, 2014). The European Union, in particular, has become a net importer of biomass and biofuels (Bourguignon, 2015) in order to meet the targets set out in the Renewable Energy Directive (2009/28/EC), which stipulated that, by 2020, 20 per cent of the energy used in the European Union and 10 per cent of the fuel for transport in each Member State should come from sources considered renewable.

Given their proximity to Europe, many African governments saw a market opportunity in European energy policies. At the same time, agrofuels began to be presented as a viable development strategy for African countries (Mitchell, 2010), although their production was practically non-existent before the 2000s (United Nations Industrial Development Organization,

2009), and several cooperation programmes were promoted, focusing on its development. Since that time, cooperation agencies, non-governmental organizations and philanthropic organizations have been engaged in exploring regulatory frameworks or mapping the agricultural potential of African lands. The emphasis on agrofuels was thus articulated with the new wave of rural development policies following the 2007–2008 crises and focused on the expansion of arable land. As we have seen, the then Senegalese president was among the most ardent promoters of this development strategy. However, the latter also complemented the economic and energy policies of other states, especially Italy's.

Growth diplomacy and failed targets

Between 2008 and 2009, Italian entrepreneurs were among the main land contractors in Senegal (Benegiamo, 2022). At least eight Italian companies were granted access to land concessions to establish agrofuel plantations. In 2016, the Land Matrix portal listed Italy as the second-largest land investor in Senegal in terms of the number of deals signed, but first in terms of the total size of land involved in the transitions (Land Matrix, 2016). Back in 2011, a report by the Italian Ministry of Foreign Affairs hailed Italy's role as the second foreign investor, writing that Italy had 'beaten even Chinese competition' (Sensi, 2012). It also reiterated the Italian government's commitment to support agreements with private companies to cultivate Jatropha for the energy market.

In fact, since the early 2000s and in the following years, the commitment of the Italian government to promote the initiatives of Italian companies in the agro-energy sector in Africa has been a constant diplomatic activity. In 2013, a study conducted by the think tank Istituto per gli Studi di Politica Internazionale (ISPI), commissioned by the Italian Ministry of Foreign Affairs, designated the African continent as a strategic area for the revitalization of the Italian economy and its companies, which had been severely affected by the economic crisis (Carbone et al, 2013). The study presented the continent as going through a dynamic growth phase, with a nascent domestic market that could offer interesting prospects for Italian companies, particularly in the field of renewable energy production. The internationalization of Italian companies in the field of renewables was also seen as an opportunity to expand Italy's diplomatic role on the continent – a strategy referred to by ISPI as 'growth diplomacy' (Carbone et al, 2013, p 89), which could give Italy a leading role 'in influencing development processes and governance on a global scale' (Carbone et al, 2013, p 89).

Senegal was among the countries that, according to the report, had the prerequisites for this 'growth diplomacy' and it is no coincidence that diplomatic exchanges with Italy have intensified since 2006. In December

2007, the Italian and Senegalese governments signed a memorandum of intent to strengthen investment cooperation in various sectors, especially in agriculture. In February 2008, Senegal hosted an exploratory mission led by a delegation of Italian investors to promote technical and scientific partnerships in the production of agrofuels (Sensi, 2012). One of the results of this initiative was the signing of a pre-agreement between the company Tozzi Renewable Energy SpA, a subsidiary of the Italian company Tozzi Green, and the then Senegalese Minister of Biofuels, which was followed by the transfer of land to the company (Sensi, 2012). The plan was presented as *best practice* at the Senegal Country Presentation, organized in Rome on 27 July 2009, by the Italian Ministries of Foreign Affairs and Economy and Finance in collaboration with the main bodies that support the internationalization of Italian companies, such as the Institute for Foreign Trade Insurance Services and the Agency for the Promotion of Italian Companies Abroad, ICE.

The agreement between the Senegalese government and the Tozzi group envisaged the gradual implementation of Jatropha cultivation, initially on 500 hectares, which were supposed to increase to 2,500 in the second year, and eventually to 50,000 hectares, for which a 99-year concession was already being negotiated (Manes and Franchi, 2012, p 19; Sensi, 2012). The area initially involved in the project was in the Tambacunda region; however, the local government's reluctance to assign the entirety of the land seems to have forced the company to negotiate its presence with the local farmers by entering into a cultivation contract with them that guaranteed Jatropha Technology Farm SARL (JTF), Tozzi Group's subsidiary in Senegal, the exclusive right to purchase the final product for a period of 45 years. However, problems soon arose both in the process of acquiring the desired areas and in the management of the project due to the low yield of crops. The company reacted by lobbying local producers for an expansion of the land concession and, at the same time, negotiating a deal for 2,000 hectares in the neighbouring rural community of Ndoga Babacar, which, once obtained, prompted the company to terminate the first agreement with the farmers. In the second location, the land had been easily surrendered as it was not cultivated; however, it belonged to a protected forest area and the company was fined for illegal logging. The difficulties encountered combined with the low productivity of Jatropha convinced the Tozzi group to withdraw from Senegal and turn to other countries, deciding however not to pursue Jatropha farming.

In addition to that of the Tozzi group, other investments by Italian entrepreneurs in Senegal were withdrawn or scaled down within a few years (Benegiamo, 2022). The investments were made between 2007 and 2009 and there seems to have been no further land initiatives by Italian companies after that. However, information is not easily accessible and there is no public data available for consultation. Two of these (the case of the company En.Cor and that of Bertola Bio Energie) were widely covered in the Italian media, as their bankruptcy had monetary repercussions on the balance sheets of two Italian municipalities. In one case, the municipality of Correggio (Emilia Romagna) was required to pay over EUR 30 million in debt incurred by En.Cor, the company for which it had stood surety in exchange for supplying biomass to municipal power plants. In the other case, the municipality of Orsona (Lombardy) owned a large share of unpaid taxes when the Bertola company went bankrupt, despite its attempts to save itself and restore profitability through land investments and reconversion in the energy sector.

The vicissitudes of Italian investments are not an isolated case. A significant aspect of the first wave of farmland acquisitions concerns the large number of failures and projects that were either withdrawn or forced to downscale the size of concessions and delay the start of production (Nolte et al, 2016). Although the role of local and global protests remains unclear, the gap between promises and reality typical of green economy rhetoric has certainly contributed to deflating the expectations of both investors and of politicians. A case in point is that of Jatropha, one of the most widespread and heavily sponsored crops in the early 2000s, when it was widely presented as a miraculous, high-yielding, low-water plant, capable of growing in arid or poorly irrigated soils. After raising many expectations, Jatropha turned out to be far less profitable than expected and was gradually abandoned as a plant from which to obtain agrofuels (Nolte et al, 2016).

Green incentives and the race of the 'newcomers'

The sudden interest of Italian entrepreneurs in the cultivation of agrofuels on African soil can be partly explained in the light of Italy's reception of the European Union's Renewable Energy Directive, which led the Italian government to adopt several measures to promote the use of renewable energy sources, mainly geared towards providing subsidies to small- and large-scale producers of energy from biomass (Carrosio, 2011). The measures adopted ranged from quota obligations to Feed-In Tariffs to tax exemptions. The latter were designed for the agro-diesel sector and were based on the reduction of excise duty on domestic production.

Those mechanisms were gradually discontinued after having been in place from 2001 to 2009, and the reduction of tax breaks for the agro-diesel sector encouraged Italian oil companies – the main customers for domestic producers – to buy on the global market. The situation is different for the energy sector and, in particular, for bioliquid and biogas power plants, whose number has been increasing since the late 1990s. However, a turning point for the sector came in 2008, with the approval of incentives for small renewable power plants (with a capacity of less than 1 MW).

First and foremost, it was the green certificate mechanism that boosted demand for bioliquids and biomass (Chiaroni et al, 2011). These are 'clean energy' certificates that can be traded and sold to third parties, especially to energy producers for whom there was a purchase obligation, according to the cap-and-trade mechanism typical of the green economy. Created in 2003, after a period in which they had settled at fairly high values, they plummeted in 2007, generating a crisis in the incentive system (Chiaroni et al, 2011, p. 50). To address the problem, the 2008 financial law introduced substantial reforms to the entire incentive system and the Gestore dei Servizi Energetici (GSE, an Italian joint-stock company controlled by the Ministry of Economy and Finance) committed to take unsold certificates off the market by purchasing them at a fixed price over two years, guaranteeing their market value and liquidity. The Finance Act also allowed small renewable plants (<1 MW or <200 kW for wind power plants) that started operation after 1 January 2008 to choose between green certificates and a new form of incentive represented by the so-called all-inclusive fixed tariff (according to the European Union's Feed-In Tariff mechanism) and valid for a period of 15 years.

Thanks to public subsidies and price guarantees (the same that African developmentalist governments were criticized for in the 1980s and blamed for the lack of economic growth), the production of green energy for the domestic market had become a very profitable business that led to a substantial increase in the number of small power plants, primarily in northern Italy, and attracted new investors to the energy sector. According to the GSE (2008), in 2007 there were less than 30 bioliquid power plants in Italy, while two years later their number had risen to almost 100 units (GSE, 2009). With 283 units, by June 2012 bioliquid power plants had almost tripled to 414 units just six months later for a total generation potential of 1,015 GWh (GSE, 2012). A number of agricultural enterprises signed contracts with Italian agrofuel producers. At the same time, owing to market volatility and the effects of the economic downturn, many distilleries had to reconvert their production processes (Monni and Stirpe, 2010).

The exponential growth of the power plants had to contend with a structural problem: the lack of raw material. As stated in a report drawn by the Italian Agricultural Mechanisation Body (Ente Nazionale per la Meccanizzazione Agricolaa [ENAMA]) (Monni and Stirpe, 2020), within the framework of the Biomass Project commissioned by the Ministry of Agriculture, Food and Forestry, the necessary raw material would not have been available even if all agricultural land on the peninsula had been allocated to energy production. The demand for crude oil to be allocated to power plants had already exceeded the annual production of oilseeds in 2009. Not to mention that all this happened right in the middle of a food crisis that saw prices of vegetable oil and raw seeds soar in global markets. Going to Africa and securing one's own supply chain could only seem a convenient choice.

Italian investments in Senegal were therefore a specific trend, and all of them initially focused on the cultivation of plants for bioenergy production, especially Jatropha. Almost all the Italian companies that invested in Senegal were also small- and medium-sized enterprises, with the exception of the Vescovini group, which includes Società Bulloneria Europea (SBE Spa with its registered office in Monfalcone), which founded SBE Senegal in 2007, in collaboration with the Italian consultancy agency Jatropha Agroils, to develop a Jatropha pilot project (EuropAfrica, 2011; Sensi, 2012).

Most of the Italian investors were also new to the renewable energy market and had no previous experience in agribusiness or agricultural production. Of all the companies involved, only three seemed to be engaged in energy-related activities before starting their Senegalese venture and had their own solid and liquid biomass plants already in place in Italy. In these cases, energy production represented a small part of the companies' business activities. It was at the beginning of the 2000s, coinciding with the Italian boom in renewables, that energy production became the main activity of these companies, sparking interest in supplying their plants with raw materials from international sources.

These included the aforementioned Tozzi Group, which also negotiated land concessions in Laos and Madagascar in the same years (Manes and Franchi). A second investment involved the Nuove Iniziative Industriali group, which in turn had attempted to obtain a total area of 80,0000 hectares across Kenya, Ethiopia and Guinea (CSI, 2013).[9] In all other cases, the investments seem to have been conducted by newcomers in the energy sector who wanted to benefit from Italian incentives for renewable energy and, perhaps, to diversify production at a time of severe economic recession. This may in fact be the case for investments led by companies whose main activities were in logistics and industrial manufacturing.

The majority of investors withdrew as economic conditions changed, including the lowering of oil prices, which put the agrofuel business on hold, and the reduction of Italian incentives. Italy has recently introduced several short supply chain proposals, although they do not seem to be operational yet.[10] As most of the critical debate has pointed out, the failure of many land investments has demonstrated the inconsistency of the populist outlook on 'pro-poor agrofuels', particularly evident among the projects based on the cultivation of *Jatropha-Curcas* that have suffered the most failures (Nolte et al, 2016). On the other hand, the eruption of conflicts and protests has largely disproved estimates of empty or available African land. With respect to this, the Italian investments affair makes it possible to highlight a further point that is often overlooked in the debate, and which concerns the role played by investors, their characteristics in terms of specific skills and capabilities, and also their perception of the investment environment. Indeed, it should not be forgotten that land deals have been strongly encouraged by governments and development actors, based on an alleged greater capacity of private capital (as opposed to governments and local producers) to solve yield problems, fill financial and technological gaps, and develop the green energy sector in 'poor and technologically underdeveloped countries'.

An emblematic failure: the Senhuile-Senethanol case

The pioneering spirit has always been part of the self-narratives of capitalism. Entrepreneurs, often described as self-made men, are presented as brilliant and determined men, endowed with innovative ideas and skills and whose enrichment is justified both by a kind of first-mover advantage and as a just reward for the risks undertaken. However, many of them act within legal and political frameworks in which the main risks weigh mainly on the people and territories where their activities take root. Senhuile, as well as other Italian investors in Senegal, has largely benefited from the rhetoric about the innovative and redeeming action of foreign investors and their crucial role as new development drivers.

In the delta, the physical distance from the water and the decrease in funds allocated to sustain agriculture had contributed to making the *jeeri* areas residual spaces in the region's economy, while excluding them from the 'modernization' efforts undertaken by the various governments in office. It is with the arrival of the 'big investors' that the hydraulic territorialization project is taken over by the state and the main development players. The region is described as an ideal territory for the expansion of agribusiness where, according to the World Bank, there might be 'parcels of land of 15,000 and 40,000 hectares which are suitable for commercial expansion' (World Bank, 2013).

The concept of availability is ambiguous to say the least and often reiterates the colonial idea of empty lands;[11] it would be more appropriate to define them as having been 'emptied' of their values for local populations and re-assembled as territories functional to accumulation. Historically, the category of empty or under-utilized land has been easily applied to grazing and pastoral territories, where the fact of rendering local uses invisible is reinforced by a discontinuous and cyclical practice of space occupation. We find it echoed in the statements of the company's chief executive officer, Tampieri who, after the Fanye tragedy and scandal, told the Italian press: '[T]he 20,000 hectares we leased are a complete desert; on that land I drove at 100 km per hour with my car because the land was completely bare, with no trees' (Calzolari, 2011).

What happens if we relate this statement to the way of inhabiting space as defined in the Fulɓe pastoral environment? At least in the context under consideration, it tends to take on highly standardized forms. The basic organizational level draws a geography that divides the territory into two distinct spheres, the first circumscribed and the second undefined. Starting from a significant point, a tree or a pond, the village, *wuro*, takes shape, around which the savannah or forest, *ladde*, extends.[12] The separation between the *wuro* and *ladde* constitutes the essential element around which the pastoral space is drawn. The *wuro* corresponds to what we may call the proper space, the *chez-soi* (Mathieu et al, 1989, p 225). The *ladde* is an ambiguous and ambivalent entity, 'savannah wilderness' and source of danger, dwelling place of the outdoors and place of solitude, but necessary and utilized as well as something that, potentially, can always be occupied and tamed (Ciavolella, 2010, p 40). The *wuro* also defines the limits of the domestic environment, within which the house is built, home to the basic family unit and normally owned by the bride, who usually provided the timber and elements needed for its construction. Bounded by an enclosure generally made of intertwined dry branches, the *wuros* are relatively small units, within which we find an average of four to five houses as well as spaces for cooking, and sometimes storage. They constitute the basic unit, the village, that is a group of families living together. Sometimes, as in the case of the reserve, the *wuro* may also be inhabited by a single family that has decided to move away from the village. Each *wuro* shares the space of an encampment with other households.

The peculiarity of the Fulɓe territory can then be traced back to the distance separating the individual villages from each other. The encampment ends up constituting a vast space, spread over several kilometres, and it is difficult to perceive it totally at a single glance. As Marguerite Dupire (1962) also explains, in addition to dwellings, the space of the *wuro* usually includes a *weendo* (a small pond) and a *toufndè* (a term designating watering points located on a lake or river), that is, a point of access to water available during the *hivernage* and at the end of the rainy season respectively. On a small clay depression, the *barjal*, a space is carved out for rain-fed millet farming, while houses are normally located on the raised sandy plains known as *seeno*. Just outside the inhabited enclosure, a series of other enclosures, this time built with thorny branches (*ngaalgu*) serve to contain the animals, which are separated by breed and sex. From each *wuro*, beaten paths lead to another village, a pond, a grazing area or into the *ladde*.

Despite its enormous dispersion and mobility, the pastoral territory thus remains a highly ordered territory, where the area occupied by the village responds to internal accommodation needs and depends on the availability of resources, the number of animals and inhabitants. Moreover, it becomes evident how both the village space and the surrounding space, the *ladde*, are important for the functioning of pastoral life and are an integral part of nomadic Fulɓe territoriality. We can imagine them as a combination of domestic space and living space and a space for life, where one is never residual in relation to the other but is always in a co-dependent relationship. The village uses the *ladde* to live and needs it to continue expanding. The *ladde* is what the village does not occupy; it exists because it is left free and vacant. It is on this 'space for life' that the Senhuile project is meant to develop, with a view to enclosing it, denying access and stopping common usage.[13]

Figure 3.1: Participatory mapping of Senhuile-Senethanol impacts on the Ndiaël Reserve

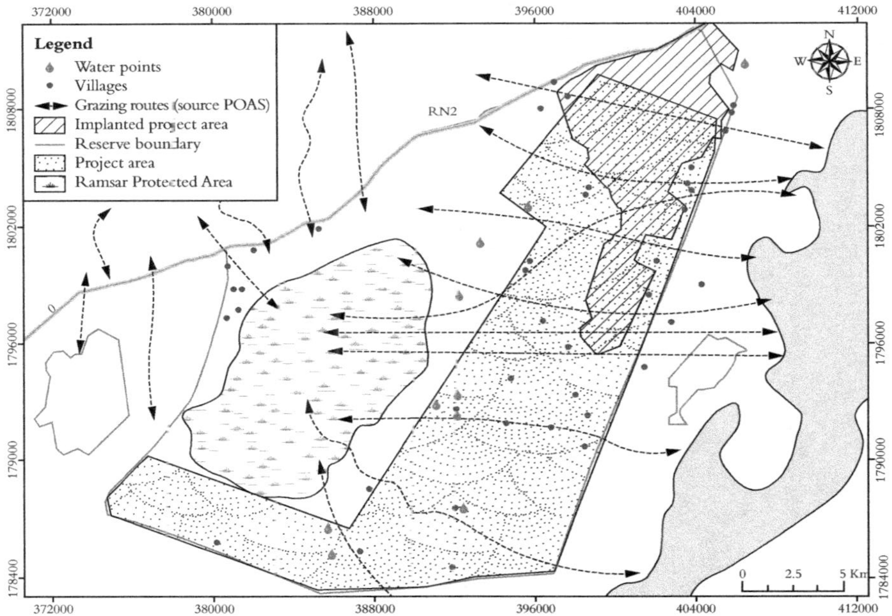

Note: Location of the Senhuile-Senethanol concession in the Ndiaël Reserve in relation to villages, water points and grazing routes.

Source: Bagnoli et al (2015, p 34). Graphic processing by Davide Cirillo. The information presented on the map was gathered through a participatory mapping activity organized by the author and Davide Cirillo in October 2014.

Figure 3.2: Aerial view of the Senhuile-Senethanol estate in the Ndiaël Reserve

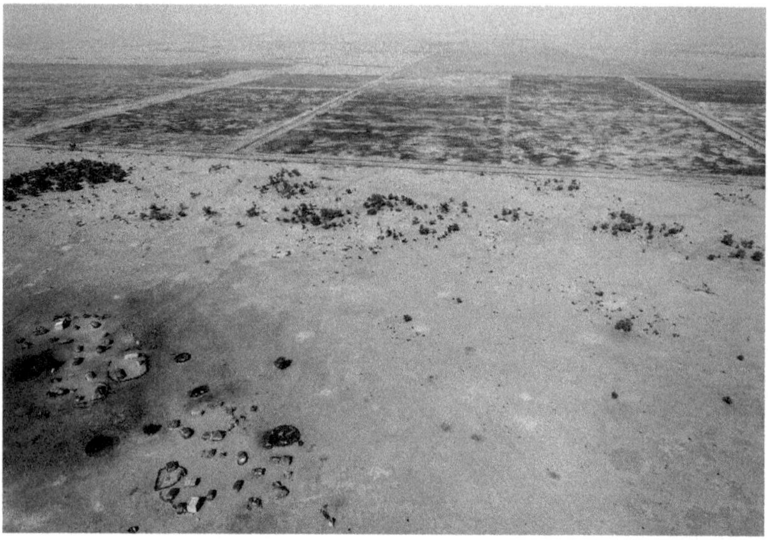

Note: Aerial photo of the Senhuile estate in Ndiaël taken in February 2014. In particular, part of the area put into production is visible, interspersed with the long open canals carrying water taken from Lake Guiers. In the background are deforested areas. Below on the left, a village, with traditional huts and some brick buildings, from which the grazing paths branch off that can be seen from above as 'lines' where the ground is more trodden.

Source: © Giada Connestari

From Italy to Senegal

When, six months after the violent clashes in Fanaye, on 20 March 2012, President Wade issued two decrees on the same day,[14] making the relocation of the Senhuile-Senethanol project official, the central government had invoked the public interest as a criterion legitimizing the expropriation in the Ndiaël Reserve. The first decree stipulated that an area of 26,550 hectares, which is part of the the Ndiaël Avifauna Reserve, should be downgraded from its protected status for reasons of public interest. The second decree allocated 20,000 hectares for a period of 50 years, renewable by tacit agreement, to the Senhuile-Senethanol group. The remaining 6,550 hectares were to be made available to the peoples of the Ngnith and Ronkh Rural Communities (since land granted is located within their respective administrative boundaries) for the reconstruction of villages that may have been displaced as activities proceeded, or otherwise earmarked for socio-economic promotion activities.[15] The allocation of these 6,550 hectares never took place: the company decided not to displace the 37 villages residing on its territory, opting for the solution of surrounding the settlements with crops, so as to leave a space corresponding to a circle with a diameter of 500 or 300 metres, depending on whether it was an official village or a small group of dwellings (*hameux*).[16]

From what has just been described, the total incompatibility between the inhabitants' use of the land and the use planned by the company becomes evident, so the decision not to relocate the villages did not prevent the company from facing local protest. The main issue is that the implementation of the project makes cattle farming impossible, and places a *de facto* limitation on the villages' ability to move and grow, which is pitted against the freedom of movement and growth of the Italian company, the project's main shareholder.

The decrees signed by Wade were issued between the two rounds of presidential elections. This move was deemed unseemly and made in haste. In the second round it was Macky Sall who won. The new president had based part of his electoral campaign against 'land-grabbing' and, thanks to this, had obtained broad support in the Ndiaël area. On 12 April 2012, Sall suspended the project with a decree.[17] Four months later, however, a second decree revoked the previous one, thus reconfirming the validity of Wade's first decrees and giving Senhuile-Senethanol's activities in the area the green light again.[18]

Although the land is entrusted to a consortium of Senegalese companies, the agricultural project is entirely defined by and refers to an Italian company: the Tampieri Group. Established in Faenza in 1928 as a company specializing in the production of crude oil from grape-seed presses, in the 1960s it also took on the production of flour for the energy, food and livestock markets. In 1996, thanks to an investment in its facilities, it started producing refined oils for food use. In 1979, it became a joint-stock company and ten years later, in 1989, it introduced sunflower processing. In 2011, the year of the investment, its production included sunflower seed and maize germ alongside the production of protein flours for livestock use, which are made from sunflower, maize germ and grape skins. Today, according to a statement on its website, the Tampieri Group is 'the leader in Italy in sunflower processing, with 250,000 tonnes/year of crushed seeds and a production of refined oil equal to 250,000 tonnes/year, more than 50 per cent of the entire national production'.[19]

The adventure in the field of renewables began a long time ago. As early as the early 1980s, the steam produced from the combustion of flours was used to meet part of the company's energy needs. Since 2001, Tampieri has been a holding company with control over four subsidiaries specializing respectively in the production of vegetable oils and flours; production of electricity from biomasses; production of bio-ceramic medical devices; water purification (also for third parties); and a real estate company dealing with logistics. The establishment of a holding company marks the start of an increase in share capital and expansion into the international market. Heliantus Srl Tampieri, an affiliated company of the group, started the production of agrofuels from vegetable oils and their distribution. The company also holds 28.10 per cent of a holding company, EN.E.R. Spa, which in turn controls four companies, all engaged in the production and trade of energy from alternative sources as well as from hydrocarbons and gas.

The first outsourcing attempt dates back to 1997, when the group created a company in Romania, AGF Cereal Rumena Srl, to secure a constant supply of raw materials: sunflower and oilseed rape, replaced in 2007 by maize, wheat and soya. In 2011, this model was reproduced in Hungary, which, like Senegal, has seen a sharp increase in land concentration over the last ten years, associated with recent large-scale agricultural investments. In Senegal, Tampieri was the majority shareholder in the Senhuile-Senethanol project. It controlled the Senhuile company whose main mission in the Ndiaël Reserve (according to what was initially stated both on the company website and in the environmental impact study [Senhuile SA, 2013]) was to obtain concessions to produce sunflowers to export to Italy with a view to implementing a strategy of vertical integration of the oil mill's activities. However, technical and ecological constraints, as well as the impact of the vocal opposition to this project, which gained international attention, caused it to fail and the Italian company to leave the country.

Prior to this, between 2013 and 2016, the company attempted to change production targets several times, experimenting with the introduction of new crops, including rice, peanuts and maize, probably to also ensure continuity of the concession, demonstrating its ability to put land into production and avoid accusations of inefficiency. Senhuile representatives stated that they would redirect production towards the domestic market to 'support the Senegalese people and government in achieving self-sufficiency in rice production' (Ndar Info, 2015). Despite this, the company never reached its full production capacity. It also seems to have conducted further negotiations in other rural communities, also in the delta area, to obtain new concessions. In particular, it appears to have been awarded 5,000 hectares in the rural community of Fass Ngom in 2015, which, however, never seem to have been put into production (Bagnoli et al, 2015, p 33).

In 2017, the combination of growing local hostility towards the project and the company's inability to put the land into production led the Italian investor to leave the area, selling their shares to the Senegalese partner (Ndar Info, 2017). Since then, there has been no further progress, nor is it possible to confirm who currently owns the Senhuile shares. The withdrawal of the Italian investor did not mean a return to the previous situation. The land is still under state control following the downgrading from its reserve protection status, while government agencies are pursuing other business ventures with new investors. A new company – Les Fermes de la Téranga, allegedly a shell company – took over the 20,000 hectares that had once been allocated to Senhuile but production has not yet taken off, apparently due to a scandal that was followed by a corruption investigation (GRAIN, 2019). Senhuile had also engaged in extensive land restructuring by deforesting certain areas and building long canals to transport water taken from the nearby Lake Guiers. The operations caused a constant impact on pastoral activities, also restricting grazing routes. The unfenced canals pose a safety risk to people and animals. To date, sadly, there have already been three cases of children drowning.

An impact study with many doubts

According to Senegalese law, Senhuile was required to prepare a socio-environmental impact study, the validation of which by a technical committee is a necessary condition and a prerequisite for obtaining authorization to start operations. Yet Senhuile's socio-environmental impact study (EIES) (Senhuile SA, 2013) was conducted after operations had already started. An initial version of the study was rejected by the competent authorities, but there is no public record of a new study.[20] The validation of the final document by the Senegalese authorities remains a mystery, as the environmental compliance certificate has never been made public. It has only been possible to view the first study, commissioned by Senhuile and conducted by an external agency licensed by the Ministry of the Environment, which examines the impact of sunflower cultivation on an initial 10,000 hectares. It merely tests the safety of a container of diesel oil and the planned runway for the aircraft used to spray fertilizer and pesticides on the land (it does not seem to be a problem that fertilizers spread in this way can also be sprinkled on houses, wells and animal feeding troughs).

On the other hand, there is no mention of the use and consumption of water resources and the drainage of both irrigation and drainage water. The latter, particularly with regard to rice production, which was introduced at a later stage, required to be channelled through suitable drainage ditches and then into backflow channels, in order to avoid both the formation of stagnation – and hence an increase in mosquitoes and the subsequent risk of infectious diseases – and the problem of the salinization of drainage water and surface aquifers. Nor is there any trace in the impact study of precise assessments regarding water consumption for irrigation. It seems that the company had neither an agreement nor a contract regulating the use of water taken from the lake and transported to the concession by means of open canals and initially distributed by sprinkling. All this in a context, that of the reserve, marked by a chronic lack of access to water for drinking and breeding, and in an environment where the evaporation rate averages 2.5 mm, reaching 6 mm or 8 mm at the height of the hot dry season (Mietton and Humbert, 1992). Compared to rainfall, this means that the water evaporating from the soil exceeds by about ten times the water absorbed by the land during rainfall, a balance that tends to remain negative throughout the year, including *hivernage* months (Mietton and Humbert, 1992).

Another major absence in the environmental assessment concerns the impact of replacing tree species and wild flora with a monoculture. In spite of this, Senhuile did not hesitate to deforest some 6,000 hectares[21] of Sahelian savannah, an action that clashes with all initiatives aimed at reforestation to combat desertification[22] and undermines the economic activities of the villages. Probably, the uprooting of tree species also had repercussions on local health; suffice it to say that the word tree (*lekky*) in *Poular* also means 'medicine' and is used to indicate both.

The environment code,[23] which governs how the study is conducted, states that environmental impacts also include social impacts, namely those on people's health and well-being and the resettlement needs that the project might cause. Emphasis is placed on impacts affecting specific population groups, including women. It also emphasizes the need for public and participatory consultation. In the case of Senhuile-Senethanol, the consultation process consisted mainly of a series of information days to highlight the project's benefits in terms of development and job creation. The realization of the investment was taken for granted and its implementation was not discussed. The choice of people invited to these meetings was not representative of all the villages concerned: most people consulted during the village meetings – held between 30 November and 2 December 2012 – lived outside the reserve, often in very remote areas (Senhuile SA, 2013). Only two villages were in the rural community of Ngith, which includes most of the inhabited territory of the reserve.

On 11 and 12 September 2013, two public hearings for the return of the study were held in the communities of Ngith and Ronkh, during which the participants from the local communities expressed great concern about the project (SAED, 2012), also reflected in the impact study, which states:

> The populations fear that one day they will be forced into the role of simple agricultural workers for the project, when the project has made cattle breeding or irrigated cultivation impossible, by grabbing all the resources (land, pasture and water) … Young people fear being hired and paid derisory wages. (Senhuile SA, 2013, p 51)

In regards to people residing within the reserve that were not consulted, the impact study found that the opposition of the local communities was a risk factor and that it required mitigation measures aimed at supporting the acceptance of the project, which was causing 'misunderstandings among certain fringes of the population' (Senhuile SA, 2013, p 50). Although these statements seem jarring, and should indeed indicate that the project might be unacceptable or problematic for these groups of people, it is worth noting that they are part of the approach the company adopted to delegitimize certain actors in local society. This is consistent with the approach previously followed by the government, where the importance of pastoralism in the delta was denied, and was conceived as a backward-looking and economically irrational practice. The environmental and social impact assessment drawn by Senhuile reads as follows:

> Many villages are predominantly Fulani and this shows that pastoralism is their *favoured* activity; it is an important sector of the local economy. However, for socio-cultural reasons, the practice of this activity does not meet economic criteria. This is why livestock farming does not occupy the place it deserves as a leading activity. Indeed, owing to the *actors' lack of professionalism*, this sector is not sufficiently open to innovation and modernisation. This is why the Senhuile project, which also brings about a change in livestock farming, is causing great concern and fear on the part of pastoralists, who cling to their traditional ways and cannot imagine any other type of cattle farming other than extensive pastoralism. (Senhuile SA, 2013, p 23, emphasis added)

Later in the text, it is announced that the changes the project plans to make are to support sedentarization and intensification of cattle farming in the Ndiaël.

Figure 3.3: Water channel constructed by Senhuile-Senethanol in the Ndiaël Reserve

Note: Canal works carried out by Senhuile in the Ndiaël Reserve. The canals, which are used to transport water for irrigation, have had a negative impact on pastoral activities, restricting grazing routes. They have also blocked normal access paths to watering points and wells used by the villages, forcing women in particular to make very long detours. The failure to secure the canals also poses a risk to the villagers and their animals. To date, three children have drowned in an attempt to cross them, play in them or collect water, as well as several animals.

Source: Author. Photo taken in April 2014.

Figure 3.4: Basic fence marking the Senhuile-Senethanol intervention zone in the Ndiaël Reserve

Note: Basic fence of the limits of the Senhuile intervention zone in Ndiaël, in the vicinity of one of the villages closest to the implemented area. The concrete post indicates the limit of cultivated plots: the company planned to leave an uncultivated space around the villages corresponding to a circle with a diameter of 500 or 300 metres, depending on whether it is an official village or an informal group of dwellings (*hameux*).

Source: Author. Photo taken in April 2014.

Figure 3.5: Deforestation work by the Senhuile-Senethanol project in the Ndiaël Reserve

Note: Deforestation work in the reserve carried out by the Senhuile-Senethanol consortium to prepare the land for sowing. In the background, a baobab tree, which can live up to 500 years and whose fruits are used for medical, nutritional and cosmetic purposes.

Source: Author. Photo taken in April 2014.

4

Conflicts in Extractive Territories

'Senhuile is worse than Ebola': implications and impact of agro-industry

On 10 September 2012, approximately 36 hours after the first trees were felled by Senhuile in Ndiaël, the inhabitants of the 37 official villages and related hamlets residing in the reserve convened a meeting in the village of Kadd Ndeff to draft a letter to be sent to the governor of the Saint Louis region (whose administration covers a large part of the delta).[1] The letter was signed by the 'Collective of the 37 villages of the Ndiaël'. From then on it was this name, and later also the name of 'Collective in defence of the Ndiaël lands', that the inhabitants of the reserve and sympathizers from the neighbouring areas used to sign a series of declarations addressed to the press, the head of state and several Senegalese ministers to demand the withdrawal of the investment and express their concern for what was described as 'a threat, if not an aggression'.[2]

The letter sent by the villagers of the Ndiaël to the governor of the region not only denounces the impact of the investment, but also declares that any possibility of negotiation between the company and the population most affected is closed. It also emphasizes the concern about the increase in social conflict generated by Senhuile's presence in the area. Indeed, President Abdoulaye Wade's decision to delocalize Senhuile's investment in the delta region did not come about in general silence: both the company and various government representatives, as well as influential Senegalese businessmen, went to great lengths to obtain the endorsement of the project by the inhabitants and the local municipal council. A series of more or less formal meetings between the latter and representatives of the company took place between the end of 2011 and the second half of 2012, during the period between the withdrawal of the decree signed by Wade and its reapproval during Macky Sall's term.

The meetings, most of which took place in Dakar, did not entail any real possibility of negotiating or rejecting the project, but rather were aimed at convincing the participants of the possible benefits of the investment. The presence of the pastoralist villages settled on the land given in concession, as well as their schools, mosques, grazing routes and watering points, was probably not seen as a real problem. Moreover, the villages were not even indicated in the project's initial maps, drawn in collaboration with the Société nationale d'aménagement et d'exploitation des terres du delta du fleuve Sénégal (SAED; Senegal River Delta Land Development and Exploitation Company) and the Saint Louis Forest Service to mark the boundaries of the actual area of the concession.

The presence of the villages is not the only missing information: the project has been characterized by a significant lack of transparency, particularly with regard to its purpose, its corporate structure and the names of the investors. Early negotiations and meetings, including those with village and rural community representatives, took place within this information asymmetry. Similarly, the research on which this book is based had to contend with the reluctance of Senhuile and Senethanol representatives to engage in dialogue and the difficulty of obtaining key information such as the text of the decrees, project maps and the environmental impact study. It was only through the combined efforts of researchers, journalists, non-governmental organizations (NGOs) and local activists that it was possible to build up an accurate picture of what was being planned in Ndiaël. These collaborations also played a fundamental role in producing a narrative that was contrary to and in conflict with the one the company had constructed about its work in the area and its relations with the inhabitants.

If land ends ...

Among the various meetings organized during the installation phase of the project, a particularly important one, but also the last, was the one that took place in August 2012 in a luxury hotel in Dakar, where village representatives sat face to face with Senhuile and Senethanol executives, in the presence of eminent businessmen close to President Macky Sall and, perhaps, of political authorities. Here, in what has come to be known as the 'Dakar compromise', the company committed itself to a series of measures, the most important of which was to halve the size of the project and move the area of interest to the buffer zone (which, however, cannot be cultivated as it is protected by the Ramsar Convention).

There is no written record of these agreements, but, as we also read in the report of the meeting for restitution to the local population[3] held two days later in the town hall of Rosso Bethio (the main town closest to Ndiaël), the representatives of the most affected villages explained the company's proposals and received an endorsement from those present to agree to the project, provided the company gave a number of guarantees, namely:

- Guarantee the local populations that their land will not be affected.
- Intervene at the level of the authorities to ensure that the state converts the forest reserve for the benefit of the population and turns it into a space for cattle and herders.
- Reassure the population that environmental standards will be met in order to contribute to the preservation of the ecology and flora needed for livestock farming.
- Ensure their participation in the delimitation of the buffer zone (the area that protects the Ndiaël *cuvette* and is not even used for grazing).
- Ensure their involvement in project management.
- Undertake that the jobs resulting from the project will be reserved exclusively for the population of the villages located in the Ndiaël Reserve.
- As agreed in the project promoters' proposal, 800,000,000f (eight hundred million CFA francs) per year will be allocated to the population, and these funds will be managed by a commission composed of the villagers themselves.
- As part of the agreement, they will commit to making 6,000 hectares of land available exclusively for local and managed livestock.
- Ensure that the area is not isolated (*enclavée*).
- The right of way will be essential to allow villagers to reach Rosso Béthio or National Road 2, as the project is located between the latter and the villages.
- Build roads leading to the villages and to the national road.
- Participate in the construction of schools, clinics and other development projects.
- Ensure water supply in the area for the people and cattle, as the project occupies water and grazing points.
- Finally, the people expressed their desire to be associated with all the company's operations in order to be kept informed of the project's direction and solve any problems that might arise as a result of these new activities.[4]

Two considerations can help us better understand the willingness to negotiate and the sense of these requests. The first concerns the population's perception of their ability to oppose and resist a project whose imposition comes directly from the state. On the other hand, since they are claiming land whose pastoral vocation tends to be considered secondary to the agricultural needs of the country, the inhabitants cannot aspire to a recognition that involves them as a specific group, distinct from the social fabric as a whole, which requires specific policies.

The right of a group of herders to refuse to make sacrifices and to oppose a project that claims to benefit the entire community is not a fact that is recognized even locally, but a political horizon that needs to be constructed.

What is more, the occupation of the last pastures marks the approach of an event that has been announced for a long time, linked to the subordination of pastureland and the lack of support for extensive livestock farming, especially at a time when the sector is undergoing a difficult transition.

In terms of these dynamics, the Senhuile project is accelerating and exacerbating the long-standing pastoral crisis in the delta. It also acts as a catalyst, triggering reactions on a variety of issues that existed before the project. These include the interpretations, reactions and strategies that the pastoralists have so far adopted to deal with the process of marginalization that has historically affected them. In this sense, the arrival of the investment is also a turning point, since it marks the exhaustion of the conditions of autonomy that have been at the centre of the resistance strategies adopted for a long time, and in a way marks a 'before' and an 'after' as to the forms of political conflict.

At a demonstration in the reserve in January 2015, residents carrying long red pieces of cloth (the colour symbolizing rejection in Senegal) marched while chanting the slogan: 'Senhuile-Ebola! Senhuile-Ebola!'. This was one of the few protests of this kind, as any request for a permit to hold a demonstration has always been refused by the authorities. So, the inhabitants opted for a march around the villages, which did not need a permit, and was broadcast live by journalists who had been contacted for the occasion. This was at the time of the outbreak of the Ebola epidemic in Africa, which attracted international attention and concentrated political efforts. The comparison with Senhuile was chosen to underline the danger of the investment: 'Who did this: it's the project (Senhuile). We don't know where we're going, it's more dangerous than Ebola.'[5] A little earlier, in another village in Ndiaël, one of the oldest in the region, a very old man, whose identity card said he was 93, told me about the situation using the phrase 'Akhir az-Zaman!', a Koranic expression comparable to the Christian apocalypse.

In this context, the question of access to land, and the sense of insecurity with which it is perceived, plays an important role, as another herder living in Ndiaël puts it:

> In terms of land, what is left [in the delta] is not enough. Wherever you put your foot, you are told to take it off because it is already reserved for someone else. So, if wherever you put your foot, you are told to take it off, then if you look closely, you realize that we are facing a big problem: we are really hanging in the balance. Because I think if you've lived in a place for more than a hundred years and you don't have any paper that can justify your ownership of that land, then you're without guarantees, you're really floating in a vacuum. So our ownership of this land is not final, because our guarantee of being here is not forever.[6]

The depletion of the space left by the agricultural advance thus marks the closure of the frontier, which is now showing its limits by becoming a largely definitive margin. The pressure on land, which has led to considerable competition, means that there is no place in the delta that is not already occupied by agriculture or the presence of other villages. Faced with the prospect of the reserve being downgraded, the pastoralists' strategies for resisting the advance of the agricultural front no longer seem viable. If the possibility of a major conversion to agro-pastoralism was possible, and for some an almost obligatory choice, during the period of great territorial transformation linked to the launch of large-scale irrigation projects, today this prospect seems difficult to reproduce, assuming it is desired. 'We'll be forced to leave because pastoralism will no longer be viable. There are lots of herds here, and we can't manage with the space that's left'; these are some of the phrases I heard repeatedly in Ndiaël during the Senhuile presence.

The problem of the impossibility of maintaining the herd in such a limited space was explained to me so often, and often by the same people, that it almost gave me a feeling of 'alienation'. Even though my questions were about opinions, aspects or implications of the investment other than its direct environmental impact, almost every conversation about or mention of the Senhuile project began with this explanation. After three years of regular visits to the reserve, I was surprised that the people I spoke to still felt the need to clarify a fact that I seemed to have amply demonstrated that I understood and shared.

In the end, I realized that it was not just a matter of repetition. The physical impossibility of the coexistence of the business project and pastoralism was somehow the underlying postulate of any possible argument about Senhuile's presence. The opinions and reactions associated with it could only be explained and their logic clarified in the light of the impossibility of finding a compromise. From the point of view of my interlocutors, the conflict is not a desired outcome, but an immediate one. The 'of peace', the 'fatigue', the 'disturbance of family harmony' are repeatedly mentioned as consequences resulting from the need to oppose the investment, but they are judged as adverse and problematic events for those who have always preferred to maintain their independence in a space of 'external marginality'[7] to large territorial structures.

'We have never asked anything of the state, we only ask that they leave us alone!', a village chief told me the first time I visited.

Pastoral subjectivities

The end of the pastoral space cannot be read solely as an economic and labour issue, as it has to do with the set of self-representations, subjectivities and choices associated with this way of life. Being a herder is not a job in the sense that this word has taken on under industrial capitalism, and despite the various changes the region has undergone over the years, the people I spoke to, as well as their grandparents and great-grandparents, had repeatedly and actively chosen to be and remain pastoralists. It was a choice that had to do with questions of identity, autonomy and sense of self. Issues that had a whole series of social and political implications that can be summed up in the idea of margin that we outlined earlier. Of course, this statement does not exclude the existence of a wide range of subjectivities, and the problem has different connotations if one is old, young or female, if one has many or few cows. In Ndiaël, all these differences exist, but they did not play a predominant role in the opposition to the project, which was unanimous.

The importance of pastoralism is also linked to traditions and the moral and behavioural codes that characterize the Fulani way of life and distinguish it from the rest of the world. While these 'codes' have been the subject of numerous debates and diatribes in the anthropological literature (Breedveld Anneke and De Bruijn, 1996), it will suffice to say that the people with whom I conducted my research in Ndiaël repeatedly mentioned the importance that virtues such as patience, decency and self-dignity had in education and social interaction. I could see this sense of decency in the relaxed faces, the calm words and the dignified glances directed at the eyes of the people they were talking to. I saw it in the appropriate and welcoming hospitality I received, and I could sense it in the relationships between adults and young people. And I certainly felt it in my interviews with some very old people.

During the different experiences I have had in non-European countries and communities with close links to indigenous traditions, I have rarely noticed the feeling of almost reverence that I believe was once felt here in Europe when in the presence of an elder. I thought about this for a long time, mainly to get rid of any lingering exoticism and not to let the feeling of disorientation at being immersed in a context so far from my own affect my analysis. In the end, I told myself that what always humbled me when I spoke and listened to the elders in Ndiaël was the fact that both their posture and their words gave me the impression, without ever actually saying so, that the speaker's self-confidence was based on a sense of belonging to a geographically and temporally vast history, ranging from the Futa Toro Empire in the central and eastern part of the Senegal River Valley to the Sokoto Empire in Nigeria and Cameroon.

This history is also enshrined in the lineage traditions and in the surnames, called *yettode*, which are always the same and remain unchanged to this day, and which refer to the four eponymous ancestors from whom all Fulɓe people are said to descend: Sow, Bâ, Barry and Jallo (or Diallo), each of whom is associated with a cardinal point, a primordial element and the colour of a cow's coat (Sow, 2001). Perhaps, I say to myself now as I write, it is this awareness of being in the presence of a person who is also, in a way, the history of his people that I have perceived the sense of belonging to the Fulani identity in many of the conversations I had while on the reserve.

There is, moreover, a sense of nobility among pastoralists that has little to do with property or monetary wealth, but rather with what was, and to some extent still is, the rigid hierarchical organization underlying *haalpulaar'en* societies (that is, of those who speak Pulaar), which distinguishes free men, classified according to their professions, from nobles (*dimo*, pl. *rimɓe*) and slaves (*maccuɓe*), who traditionally work the fields. Within this organization, as the anthropologist Riccardo Ciavolella has explained, the combination of profession and 'ethnic identity' gave rise to the noble status; one could therefore say that in Fulɓe societies there was 'a coincidence between three characteristics: to be Fulani (Fulɓe) in the ethnic sense, to be noble (Aynaaɓe) in the social sense and to be pastoralist (Rimɓe) in economic activities' (Ciavolella, 2010, pp 58–59). 'You see us dressed like this. You may think we are poor, but we're not. It is our way of life. You may see someone well dressed and with an expensive car, but it is possible that he is poorer than I am',[8] I was once told, which reminded me of the criticism I sometimes heard in Senegal about the Fulani, who are often accused (and in various African countries are often the victims of ethnic racism) of not knowing how to make the most of their wealth.

As an element of prestige and a marker of 'Fulanity', the cow also occupies a central place in Fulɓe socio-cosmogony. Tierno Monénembo, a Guinean writer, begins his novel *Peuls* (2004) with a reflection that recounts the genesis of the Fulɓe people and clarifies the fundamental link between the Fulani and cattle:

> In the beginning was the cow. Guéno, the Eternal, created the cow first. Then he created the woman, and only after that he created the Fulani. He placed the woman behind the cow. He put the Fulani after the woman. This is what the genesis of the herder says, this is what the holy trinity of the herder does. (Monénembo, 2004, p 11)

He continues:

> The Fulani says: the cow is superior in the services it renders to all the works of creation. The cow is magic, more magic than fairies! She appears, and the desert blooms again. She moos, and the Reg [stony desert] softens. She snorts and the cave lights up, nourishes, protects, guides. She shows the way. She opens the gates of destiny. (Monénembo, 2004, p 12)

The idea of the importance of pastoralism for identity is also supported by the special relationship that traditionally exists between the herder (*gaynaako*) and the cow (*nagghe*), which is expressed in a form of common kinship between the herder and the herd and formalizes a distinction between cows according to different 'lineages' of belonging: on the one hand, those that have been linked to the owner or his family for several generations, and on the other, 'exogenous' cows acquired through a process of absorption that devalues them in the eyes of the owner (Ciavolella, 2010, p 52). A reciprocal descent that shows how the relationship between herder and animal is not one of ownership in the sense of mere possession, but of mutual co-ownership, as described in this very famous song sung by the Fulɓe of the Futa Djallon, in Guinea, and also quoted by Monénembo in his novel:

> God has the whole universe, the Fulani has cows.
> The savannah has elephants, the Fulani has cows.
> The cliff has monkeys, the Fulani has cows.
> The moorland has deer, the Fulani has cows.
> The sea has waves, the Fulani has cows. (Monénembo, 2004, p 7)

If the Fulani and their cattle form a systemic whole, and it is the animal that makes the *pullo* (singular of *fulɓe*) what he is, the centre of this cosmogony is represented by milk, the main element of exchange, the trading or bartering of which traditionally falls to women (see, for example, Kettel, 1992; Shehu and Hassan, 1995).

In fact, it is said that the world was created from a drop of milk (Beier, 1966, pp 1–2). In the same way, as was explained to me during an interview in Ndiaël, in order to understand the crisis of the pastoral economy, it is not so much the cow itself but the milk it produces, as this extract from the interview shows:

> Our core 'business' is livestock farming. What we all remember has always been livestock farming. It's what we lived on, our lives depended on it; we practiced agriculture, but not much: cattle farming was the dominant activity, really. It was through cattle farming that we got milk. We gave it to our women, who went to barter for it. By selling milk, some people were able to solve their problems [*Ena wadi ko yéyé-tè, diéyadam niawda hadiouma goto*. Literally: the milk is there, you sell it and you solve a problem]. What made life possible for us was milk. Milk was what we lived on. That was life in the past. The savannah (*ladde*) was vast, you could go anywhere you wanted. That was our life: livestock farming, since agriculture was not practiced much; our strength was livestock farming. The strength of livestock farming was milk. We lived on milk and our whole life was based on milk. From that time when the *ladde* started to shrink, the cultivated space was not enough for us. The cows did not produce milk any longer, at least not in large quantities, and that's when our problems began. Because before, even if you only had a few cows, it didn't matter how many you had,

> you could live on those few cows. Now all that has gone. Now you can have hundreds of cows, but they are of no use to you. The reason for this is that the space (*ladde*) no longer exists, the *ladde* is shrinking. Our assets [the animals] can no longer feed themselves as they used to, and they no longer give milk. We have the impression that everything has changed compared to the old days, because in the past, whatever happened with our herd, we could live a peaceful and quality life. The *ladde* is getting smaller and smaller and now we are surrounded. We are surrounded because where you used to be able to graze your cattle [the verb used here is *harnoudè*, which means 'graze until the cow has had enough'], you now have to make a detour. Wherever you want to graze, you have to take long detours to get there.[9]

'We are here for the development of Senegal': private governance and social responsibility

When Senhuile's representatives do not simply deny the company's diatribes against the local population, they usually say that it is all due to 'irrational prejudices' against the project, based on a lack of knowledge or manipulation by some of the actors involved. The problem, according to Senhuile and its spokespeople,[10] is that no one has taken the trouble to 'reassure' and 'explain' the benefits that its action will bring to the area, which should result in job offers (which were going to be minimal and subject to disputes and strikes, partly because the company would not have been able to put land into production) and various charitable activities. These range from charitable activities (distribution of fodder, medicines or boots) to providing support to small development projects, on the basis of which the company has tried to build a local consensus, but which do not seem to have achieved any real improvement in the living conditions of the population and have not addressed the problem of the impact of the agricultural project or alleviated the concerns of the local population.

These actions, which are central to the construction of the company's image, can be attributed to two rather typical dynamics in the relationship between citizens and extractivist companies, which are common to many environmental conflicts. The first expresses a general tendency for capital to intervene in marginal spaces under the guise of development and philanthropy. The second implies a governmental management of the conflict, based on the invisibilization and hierarchization of local knowledge, in which the notion of 'stakeholder' becomes crucial.

Narratives that matter

Senhuile's many community activities fall under the umbrella of corporate social responsibility (CSR). They were initially managed by the NGO

Friends of Africa,[11] whose director is the same as Senhuile's, and were subsequently integrated into the company with the creation of a CSR and communications department assisted by an Italian manager.

The creation of a dedicated department coincided with the dismissal of Senhuile's former director general in May 2014, who was replaced by a trusted employee of the Italian company, who set up a new team with Italian staff in key positions. The handover followed an international campaign by a group of NGOs to withdraw the investment. By October 2014, the initiative had collected more than 105,000 signatures and attracted some attention in Italy, preceded by the publication of a report on the Tampieri Group's investment and some of the irregularities that had been perpetrated up to that point.[12]

The situation inherited by the new general manager was therefore rather problematic: on top of a non-existent agricultural production, there was unfavourable international public opinion and persistent rejection at the local level. As the chief executive officer himself stated in an interview, 'if a bad reputation hurts big groups like Nestlé, imagine a small family business'.[13] As a reaction, the new management opted for a change of course from what had been undertaken till then, breaking the wall of silence that had shrouded the company in its early years, due to the total absence of communication not only to residents, but also to a wider public.

With the change of management, the company responded to the accusations made against it through a communication campaign based on the massive use of social networks and the distinction between a 'before' and an 'after' in Senhuile's history. The 'before' corresponds to the management, described as disastrous and catastrophic, of the former chief executive officer, who is seen as the main person responsible for the behaviour that led to the accusation of land-grabbing. The 'after' coincides with the new management, which has stated that it intends to correct its position.[14]

The entire communication campaign launched by Senhuile is a clear use of CSR as a counter-communication tool (Vanhamme and Grobben, 2009) to influence the public opinion of the Senegalese people and of potential financial actors interested in buying the investment. The preferred channel was the company's Instagram page, which is now closed. Here we find a kind of translation into images of the slogan originally adopted by Senhuile and displayed at the top of its website: 'A dream come true, cultivating in the Sahel' (the previous version read: 'A dream come true, growing sunflowers in the Sahel'). The photos published convey an emotional content that seems aimed at creating a kind of empathy with a project that is presented as a dream shared by Italian entrepreneurs and local people who are jointly committed to its realization.

The images, taken from the local area, show smiling women and children with wide eyes looking to the future, horizons and sunsets over cultivated fields, or close-ups of shimmering corn cobs, often harmoniously framed with blurred contours. A second message is that the company has strong ties to the local socio-historical context. These links are also realized through the implementation of development micro-projects, which are extensively documented and presented almost as if their importance to the company were on a par with agricultural production. Senhuile, almost humanized in this content, presents itself as something much more than an agricultural company for export; its commitment to the territory suggests that the company's interest comes after, or at least is compatible with, the pursuit of well-being, happiness and harmony rather than profit. In line with this self-image, Senhuile's chief executive officer stated in an interview that if he could define his company in three words, they would be 'development, innovation and integration',[15] qualities that he believes have enabled Senhuile 'to make a significant contribution to the well-being of the communities affected by the project'.[16]

In his study on the oil activities of the Ente Italiano per gli Idrocarburi (ENI) in the Val d'Agri, Basilicata, the Italian anthropologist Enzo Vinicio Alliegro (2012) identified two key mechanisms for understanding entrepreneurial action in contested extractive territories. The first is a kind of 'identity mystification' in which the company presents itself as the bearer of a local and international interest, focused on development and pursued on the basis of the supposed homogeneity with what it identifies as 'its territories' of belonging. The second is the 'programmatic concealment' of the overall project that the company has in mind for the territories concerned, and thus of its own development prospects. If, in the case of ENI in Basilicata, it was a question of negotiating the acceptance of each individual well without revealing the real ambitions regarding the total amount of oil that was expected to be extracted from the field and in how many years, in the case of Senhuile, the discreet implementation of deforestation and cultivation activities has the effect of delaying the evidence of major impacts and is accompanied by an attempt to gain acceptance for the project and, in the meantime, to isolate the opponents.

The process of concealment, however, was based on an attempt to silence and make invisible a local protest that had arisen in the immediate area. This attitude became a constant in the relationship between the company and the local people, whose accusations or concerns were always minimized and discredited as mere fears and superstitions. An example of this is the issue of chemical additives used in the harvesting process, which has led to a series of arguments and disagreements between the company, journalists, NGOs and local people.

Farmers in the Ndiaël region, ever mindful of the widespread cattle deaths in the 1950s caused by certain products dumped into the Guier lake by the Compagnie Sucrière Sénégalaise (a sugar cane producer that currently owns 12,000 hectares in the nearby town of Richard Toll, see Figure 3.1), have repeatedly accused Senhuile of pollution. The allegations have been taken up and publicized by journalists and NGO activists. Senhuile responded by claiming that it had only used an organic fertilizer, downplaying the residents' concerns and using this to discredit the other allegations by putting them on the same level of flimsiness. The farmers, however, denounced two things: the fear of possible water contamination and the use of an aeroplane to spread the fertilizer, and thus the lack of control over the fallout of the fertilizer, which was in fact poured over their heads. Senhuile's statements do not resolve or answer the questions raised, they do not refer to any impact studies that can assure the absence of risk. It is essentially a statement that requires an act of trust, discredits local knowledge and creates a hierarchy of 'credibility' that indicates who has the right to be taken seriously.

New social contracts: memoranda of understanding

In general terms, when a company refers to its corporate social responsibility, it is trying to take responsibility for the impact of its actions on the rest of society. It is a practice that is not regulated by law and can be defined on a voluntary basis, sharing a factual rather than a legal approach with the neoliberal governance perspective. It follows that there is no single definition of responsible business practice; it is called good practice when it succeeds and bad practice when it does not.[17] It would be a mistake, however, to dismiss the use of CSR as mere *maquillage*, especially in view of the process of institutionalization that the concept has undergone since the 1980s, a period in which its gradual integration into the dynamics of development has profoundly changed the relations between the business sector, public institutions and civil society (Scherer and Palazzo, 2011).

The progressive legitimization of CSR has played an important role in the development context. The assumption of responsibility by companies has led both to a greater awareness of their impact and to the progressive assumption of roles and functions, mostly outside of production. These have had, and continue to have, an important influence on the processes of governmentalization of territories and conflicts. The very emergence of the idea of responsible business stems from the progressive erosion of state control over the dynamics of development and over companies themselves, in a context where the process of liberalization, which began in the 1970s and accelerated in the 1990s, went hand in hand with the deregulation of the economy from a bureaucratic and regulatory point of view. The enormous mobility of capital, and therefore of companies, has allowed them to choose between different tax regimes, labour policies and environmental regulations, creating intra-state competition that has turned out to be a downward game.

Deregulation is also one of the dynamics underlying the emergence of what sociologist Ulrich Beck (1992) has called the 'risk society' and which has led to calls for new forms of global governance. Towards the end of the 1980s, the emergence of an organized civil society, including at the global level, and the growing importance of NGOs, led to the proliferation of protest campaigns that pointed the finger of blame at large international corporations for the lack of governance and human rights abuses in the countries where they operated.

Not only were multinationals held responsible for situations from which they benefited more or less indirectly, but they were also called upon to provide solutions to the problems caused by their production model (De Bakker and Den Hond, 2008). Somehow, the idea was accepted that it was up to the large corporations to bridge, on their own initiative, the gap between the expectations of a global, and especially Western, public opinion and the precarious situations of the contexts and communities in which they operate. In addition to activities that are more closely related to managing the impact of their work, companies have also taken a number of other actions aimed at providing basic services that are not guaranteed by the state. In Senegal, as in many other low-income countries, it has become common practice for companies to finance the construction of schools or local clinics, or to subsidize cooperation projects, including through organizations or foundations that carry out activities on their behalf.

All this has contributed to CSR taking a central place in corporate governance strategies. NGOs themselves began to see corporations as possible allies in promoting change and encouraging the adoption of public policies, and entered into cooperation agreements with them that were not exempt from accusations of identity or green-washing. Through CSR, multinationals have begun to integrate this new role as political actors and promoters of global governance standards into their corporate governance systems, to the extent that corporate responsibility is sometimes referred to as corporate citizenship (Matten et al, 2003). In a way, it is possible to trace in this process the emergence of large philanthropic capitalist foundations and their legitimization, such as the Bill and Melinda Gates Foundation, in which large economic groups finance social and development policies and seek to influence political decisions.

Senhuile's recourse to CSR principles went hand in hand with a campaign of interventions aimed at countering the protests of the local population. The company's actions were not limited to minimizing or concealing the protests, but were often helped by the police, who intervened to control possible riots and arrested some residents accused of sabotaging the company's machinery. The invisibility and criminalization of the protesters, which is very common in environmental conflicts and against extractivist companies, contributed to the exclusion of the collective of the 37 villages and their inhabitants from the list of favoured subjects in the social relations of the company, which preferred to deal with the populations living around the concession. This attitude was reinforced by the refusal of the inhabitants of Ndiaël to open up to cooperation with Senhuile.

In this framework, an important role is played by the signing of two memoranda of understanding (*protocoles d'accord*),[18] which are the result of a series of informal relationships maintained in the area and which, in turn, convey the involvement of the villages in the development projects set up by Senhuile. Memoranda of understanding are genuine acts of governance, usually designed to bind public and private actors to each other. The signing of these agreements is an established practice, encouraged by development and territorial governance policies that favour decentralized and multi-actor management. Widely implemented, they are referred to as best practices and constitute the main axis of regulation between the company and the territory in many extractive projects. They consist of a set of measures that mutually involve companies and citizens, who are involved in their capacity as 'interested' or 'stakeholder' subjects.

However, the success of these practices depends on legitimizing the 'validity' of the various stakeholders and their demands or concerns, which is usually done by the company. Failure of the recognition process can result in a part of the population being reduced to a state of invisibility. Memoranda of understanding between companies and local communities are particularly problematic for communities affected by investment projects, but as Peter Newell writes, 'are rarely identified as legitimate stakeholders by business and lack sufficient influence within government policy making to articulate and defend their concerns' (Newell, 2012, p 102).

We could define the partial contracts that populations sign with companies as new social contracts, concluded on the basis of a promise of development, which contribute to characterizing extractive spaces as distinct governed territories. In the case of the villages concerned with the Senhuile project, contracts are not concluded with each individual citizen or with a broad and inclusive notion of the people, but with population groups understood as 'village' and 'stakeholders'. The relationship with the company is all the more necessary because, due to the withdrawal of the state, the company is presented as the only interlocutor between the population and its political representatives. Moreover, isolated from the mediation of the state and unable to use formal channels of protest, they must also deal with all the inhabitants of the area, who are equally legitimate interlocutors, legitimized by the company entrusted with the management of the space in question.

Stakeholders by necessity?

On the day the agreements were to be signed, at a ceremony held in the base that Senhuile had built in the concession, and in the presence of the governor of Saint Louis, some bystanders, mostly from the Ndiaël area, were turned away because they did not want to sign the agreements. According to the governor, only those who accepted the investment were allowed to attend the ceremony.

The Senhuile memorandum of understanding were signed for the villages of Ronkh and Ngith by the former chief executive officer and by representatives of the Collectif des populations des villages environnants (Collective of people from the surrounding villages), which was set up for the occasion. The number and names of the villages belonging to these collectives have not been made public; they are mentioned as the villages listed in a document attached to the minutes, which, if it exists, is not available. Thanks to fieldwork, it has been possible to reconstruct much of the history and composition of these collectives.

Despite the triumphalist tone of the articles that appeared the next day in local and national newspapers announcing the pacification of relations between the company and the territory, hostility towards the company had not diminished at all, and it was coming from more and more Ndiaël villages. Uninterested in the company's offers, the villages of the reserve, which were excluded from signing the Ngnith agreement, called it 'an act of war on the part of the government'. The collective declared that it was not represented by the signatory of the protocol and denounced the signing as a hoax.

The people of Ronkh, who were less affected than the villages in the reserve because they were outside the Senhuile concession, initially joined the protests, rejecting the project and taking part in the joint meetings organized to promote mobilization. Later, however, they were more open to dialogue and joined the collective that signed the memorandum of understanding. There are a few main reasons for this change of direction, which do not cover all the motivations, but which were repeated several times in the various interviews and informal conversations. According to a member of one of the signatory villages in Ronkh, the acceptance of dialogue with Senhuile was motivated by the impossibility of rejecting a project imposed by the state and the hope of benefiting from the investment. The sense of powerlessness was reinforced by the fear that a possible refusal could result in the cancellation of agricultural concessions for village families.

In contrast to the pastoralist villages in the reserve, the Fulani villages in the Ronkh rural community practice a more integrated form of agro-pastoralism, cultivating land concessions within the agricultural perimeters established by the government on their former grazing lands. Although they are not far from the Fulani villages in the reserve, their strategies for adapting to the agricultural development of the delta were different. This overlaps with other specific features in the history of these villages, in particular their relationship with the local religious elites. Indeed, it is no coincidence that one of the first social actions undertaken by both the old and the new management was the restoration of the mosque and, later, the Koranic school. However, accepting to negotiate with the company did not fail to create bitter family divisions among those who felt they should insist on rejecting the project. Some people said that they finally gave in out of the need to restore peace.

In two memoranda of understanding, Senhuile also promised to give 0.3 hectares to families from the signatory villages. It appears that a total of about 189 hectares have been distributed by Senhuile to families living in the area.[19] Specifically, 114 hectares were allocated to the Ronkh community and 75 to the Ngnith community. The choice and the way in which the land was distributed seem to be more related to the practice of favouritism than to a genuine policy of social responsibility. Moreover, since the company had no knowledge of the practices and identities of its interlocutors, it cannot be ruled out that the beneficiaries of the concessions belonged only to the families of the signatories of the protocols. However, it is unclear under which law Senhuile is entitled to distribute land.[20] While there are doubts about the legality of this practice, the distortion and precariousness of land management is clear.

In a context such as Senegal's, where the discipline of land management is controversial and where substrata of customary law persist and sometimes prevail over positive law, a further level of paralegal complexity is added when the company itself becomes the holder of an allocation right. Apart from these land distributions, the text of two memoranda of understanding is quite limited in terms of the company's contribution to the communities, and focuses more on drawing up a series of agreements that commit Senhuile to protecting its concession. For example, a commitment to fence its fields with barbed wire, close access to crops or prioritize the sale of agricultural by-products to local people.

Senhuile's social strategy would have the effect of creating a second 'encirclement' around the villages of Ndiaël, no less important than that desired by the company with its territorialization plans. We can speak of a 'circle of consensus', albeit a precarious and negotiable one, with which the company hoped to isolate the pastoral populations living in its concession, breaking any bonds of territorial solidarity and gradually gaining ground. In fact, the company sought to broaden the base of its consensus by trying to involve more and more villages in its social activities. A practice that could be defined as a 'policy of co-optation', but which could also be interpreted as a kind of moral blackmail, since only those villages that prove to accept its presence by ceasing hostilities are entitled to the benefits and distribution of goods that Senhuile bestows on the territory.

This dynamic, which follows a geography consistent with the company's territorialization process, shows how the transformation of subjects and populations into stakeholders takes a different path, using the idea of development and the common good or general interest in different ways, reproducing approaches to inclusion and exclusion similar to those in which state power is exercised. In the case of Senhuile, the company operates at a local level (that is, both between rural communities and within the community itself, as in the case of Gnith), a division between those who, less affected by the project, can hope to benefit from it and those who, on the other hand, will not have this opportunity. The fact that the most affected populations are also the most marginalized has contributed to their exclusion, both from consultation processes and from relations with the company, which has instead sought to build its social base outside the concession, in the surrounding villages. This has enabled the company to begin to install itself and continue to seek consensus as it approaches the interior villages.

A broadening perspective

The imbalance of interests between the different inhabitants inside and outside the reserve, crystallized in the memoranda of understanding that included some villages to the exclusion of others, has contributed to accentuating herders' marginality, exacerbating existing power asymmetries and creating new hierarchies in the territory.

The way in which this has happened points to the distortions inherent in the mechanisms of neoliberal governance and the way in which they produce a fragmentation of the social fabric that can either reproduce existing cleavages, exacerbate them or create new ones. Moreover, now that they are closely involved in the territorialization of agriculture, it is no longer the state that is responsible for managing the 'development project', but a private company.

The possibility of inclusion is really an offer of a job as an agricultural worker. This is a prospect that the company promises but does not deliver, and which must be put into the perspective of the expectations of the territory. Although it is true that unemployment also affects the pastoral world, which is therefore interested in and supportive of new employment opportunities, the desire to become an agricultural worker is seen as a last resort in the face of the destruction of working conditions and the plundering of the means of production. In the interviews conducted, many people stated that they did not want to become 'agricultural workers'. The reasons for this statement are related to the desire to maintain independence and control over their working conditions, and thus to preserve pastoral practices. Consequently, it is the support of the local economy rather than an employment policy that is most desired. However, maintaining the former requires access to the territory. The central issue, which is always evaded, is that maintaining pastoralism on a small scale requires investment, particularly in fodder, and in appropriate facilities.

The cession of 20,000 hectares to Senhuile-Senethanol marks the explosion of the contradiction that underlies the precariousness of pastoralism on the

Ndiaël Avifauna Reserve land and, from the government's point of view, heralds the completion of the process of 'modernization' and agricultural expansion that has been underway since independence. From this point of view, what is read in the territory as a catastrophic and deadly event, comparable in severity to an epidemic, is understood in the discourses conveyed by the company and the government in terms of a problematic coexistence between pastoralism and development, rather than as a condemnation of pastoralism or an impossible coexistence between the two activities.

The identification of Senhuile and its work with development is not only actively promoted by the company in the construction of its image and the way it presents itself to the territory, but it is the very discourse underlying the new agricultural policies, based on attracting investment and transferring land, in Africa as in Senegal, that is driving this rapprochement. For its part, the prospect of development for pastoralism manifests itself in the need to adapt and modernize the sector through its progressive industrialization. This implies a shift from extensive livestock farming to sedentary, highly mechanized livestock farming geared towards market integration through the direct monetization of livestock capital (sale of cattle). However, this interpretation not only lacks an understanding of the pastoral economy and its internal rationality (in which the extensive and conservationist logic of cattle farming is not a mere whim, but rather a productive strategy based on optimizing resources and preserving 'fixed capital'), but is not even accompanied by adequate support:

> It is the government, not the company, that should give us strength. They said they were going to set up milk collection centres, they should do that. If they want the animals to produce milk and if they want to buy it, they should help us get more feed, but none of this has happened. We really have no help. The help they give to the farmers, if they did the same for us, we would be really strong. My idea is that they should help people to have the means to work. Helping people means giving each activity its share and its value, whether it is agriculture or pastoralism. I have seen projects for agriculture, but I have never seen projects for livestock, at least not here, and they should be carried out. In the same way that you draw up charters [give rights] for agricultural land, you should do the same for pastoralism. There should be reserved areas for both activities. They should say: this is for agriculture, this is for pastoralism. They must also give us the means, and by that we mean factories [milk storage centres]. If the factories come, and they come where the cows are, then people will be able to work; every day we will wake up, we will have work to do, we will get up and be active, and with the milk we sell we will be able to solve our problems, and all this is very important for the country. This is my idea, really.[21]

In Pulaar there is no word that exactly follows the meaning of the term 'development' as it is understood in the context of capitalist development. To speak of 'development' and 'development projects', the term *bamtima* or *bamtare* is generally used, meaning 'successful' or 'succeeding' in the sense of success, with failure as its correlate. The expression 'modernizing pastoralism', which is the way the development imperative is translated in government texts and political discourses directed at pastoralism, is instead rendered by the term *waɓelima*, which means 'change'. The local reception of the imperative to adapt to a modernizing world is thus resolved in the exhortation: *le Peul doit changer* (the Fulani must change).

Neither the word *waɓelima* nor *bamtima* contains a temporal component that refers to the idea of a 'before' and an 'after' organized along an evolutionary line, a nuance of meaning that instead remains underlying the idea of modernity or development. The change thus imposed is then read as a difficult challenge to which the pastor is called to respond. One early afternoon, as we waited for the boys to return from grazing and the girls to leave school, Amadou explained to me that it was no longer possible to survive by continuing to farm as they had always done, and he added: 'We want to change, we are not against development, but we cannot do everything at once, we need our time.'[22]

Our dialogue continued:

M: What do you mean by change?
A: The future is pastoralism and agriculture together. We need agriculture to produce fodder if we cannot graze. But it is difficult. Everywhere you turn, agriculture has priority over pastoralism, for which there is nothing.
M: If you start producing your fodder locally and therefore on a small area, does this mean you will have to reduce your herd?
A: Yes, certainly. That must be done for sure.
M: I see, but does that mean you will sell cows? I mean, will you sell more than you do now?
A: This is difficult, the Fulani is not used to this, we are not used to this.[23]

Talking to the people of the reserve, the poverty to which development is supposed to provide a solution takes on two different connotations. It has political origins and depends on constraints that are seen as 'external' to pastoral life, but on which pastoral life depends. It is the structural conditions of pastoralism that are called into question, not pastoralism itself. The figure of the 'poor herder' is used to express powerlessness, especially powerlessness to influence political decisions in one's favour. But when we talk about the life of the herder and its implications, a different discourse is adopted.

S: Our project is pastoralism.

M: But you also see how the state has another idea and also that there is very little space.

S: When you hear that, it is the owners of the cultivated fields [who say that]; it is they who want to cultivate the *ladde*. They think breeding is industrial, but we, too, think, and we think that pastoralism is in the *ladde* and in keeping the cows here or there.[24]

As has been said, giving up, by selling or reducing the herd, is a risk in the Sahel where, as a general rule, if it doesn't rain, you don't eat, and it is a huge risk for a pastoral society whose main asset is cows. If we are to take the local politicians at their word, this means entering the modern world with empty hands, a modern world that is certainly not one of abundance. 'It is easy for people to say that we need to increase sales, but I would never take it upon myself to say to this or that farmer: sell all your cows', commented a researcher from the French Agricultural Research Centre for International Development during an interview.

Paying attention to the subjectivities and subjective motivations expressed by herders, together with and beyond direct effects such as the loss of access to resources, allows us to better understand the meaning of the consequences of the new investments in the delta. In the dialogues held with people, women and men, living in the Ndiaël, the Senhuile problem is the problem of pastoralism, the reduction of space, the impossibility of participating in national life through the Fulani-pastoralist position, and the impending change, which turns out to be potentially tragic. The incompatibility of the 'Fulani position' with respect to the ongoing economic development gives rise to two considerations.

The first has to do with the idea that the processes of land centralization and accumulation in which the Ndiaël Reserve is involved, and within which the pastoral question arises, can and must be understood in terms of the production of subjectivity. The second has to do with the fact that in the forms of resistance to 'modernity' and its hierarchies, there are processes of radical reconnection of what capitalist development has helped to divide and conceal, separating the possibility of caring for a place from the capacity for social and economic reproduction of a community; making invisible the multiple histories, practices and relations that keep territories alive. 'Everything you see is based on the cow', a herder told me.

It is not only a question of resisting the processes of plunder and impoverishment, but also of bringing back to the centre narratives capable of bringing into play the other stories that inhabit modernity; in short, it is a question of the possibility of broadening our perspective and decolonizing our gaze. As someone once said to me in Ndiaël: 'Pastoralism is fragile, it counts for nothing, but if they have not seen the benefits of this activity, at least we did see them.'

Conclusion: Pastoral Futures in Dialogue with Environmental Justice

Although it failed, the project to allocate part of the Ndiaël Avifauna Reserve to agro-intensive exploitation remains a priority in local development plans. This confirms that the phenomenon of land-grabbing cannot be traced back to a single decision to grant a concession or a single land privatization, understood as an event in itself. Rather, it outlines a process, albeit a long one, of redefining relations between subjects, rights and territories, the course of which, in the Senegalese case, will also depend on the ability to build and strengthen alliances between peasant and pastoralist groups at local, regional and national levels in order to secure recognition of pastoralist land rights. Recognition has also been made urgent by the launch of a national land reform process that has gained momentum in Senegal since the early 2000s, precisely in relation to the opening up to foreign investors advocated by the new agricultural policy (Benegiamo, 2020). Today, the reform process is led by the World Bank, as a result of the Projet de Développement Inclusif et Durable de l'Agribusiness au Senegal (PDIDAS; Sustainable and Inclusive Agribusiness Development Project of Senegal),[1] launched in 2016, which aims to make 10,000 hectares of land in the delta available for the arrival of foreign investors and the development of commercial horticulture.

Although the project was still at an early stage in terms of 'valorizing' the land identified and providing work for the rural communities that have ceded it, it had developed a method of land management for investment, based on a cadastral register, which, if extended to the whole country, would, according to the Bank, make it possible to implement '*une réforme foncière en douceur*' (World Bank, 2019, pp 16 and 30). That is, the possibility of changing land control in the absence of conflict. This is indeed the response of the main development agencies, which, faced with the growing protests against land-grabbing, have turned to forms of land regulation and investment management designed to guarantee a 'win-win' solution. The PDIDAS land management system was designed precisely on the basis of the difficulties experienced in the Senhuile case, but this has not prevented the Bank from encountering local protests, particularly in the case of the pastoral areas targeted by the project.

Meanwhile, despite many withdrawn or suspended investments, the pace of global land concentration does not seem to be slowing down. For example, from 2016 to 2020, the Land Matrix portal reported 536 new cases of international transactions for agricultural or agro-energy purposes, totalling 14,477,125 hectares, of which about half, 7,803,927, were located in sub-Saharan Africa (with 212 new cases reported). Sub-Saharan Africa is thus confirmed as the leading continent in terms of the number and size of land transactions, followed by Eastern Europe (158 reported cases on 2842,892 hectares, also in the 2016–2020 period).

In this context, sectoral interventions, such as the recognition of land rights for pastoralists in Senegal, while important, risk proving insufficient without a radical questioning of the development project as a whole. Rather than seeing local conflicts as signs of mismanagement of land transactions that need to be better regulated, this book has raised the question of how land and resources are incorporated in the context of neoliberal development, and what social organizations such incorporation requires in order to function. It has done so from a political ecology perspective that sees new agricultural investments as signs of ongoing transitions aimed at defining the evolving relationship between capital, nature and society in the context of the ecological crisis. In this respect, the whole story of the Senhuile investment has made it possible to highlight certain tendencies of green capitalism, as well as its deep colonial bearing, which reappears with greater insistence precisely in the context of development.

As a matter of fact, most recent land acquisitions have found their place within energy transition policies and climate change mitigation objectives, linked to or implemented by food security policies and growth-oriented development guidelines. These policies are interrelated both in their definition of the problem and in their respective attempts to address it. The perspective of global food security has thus aligned itself with the central tendencies of green rhetoric, redirecting growth towards the possibility of renegotiating limits, denying any possible truly reflexive attitude towards the origins of crises, while trivializing the risks of such operations.

Justified by the need to preserve 'a certain way of life' (see also Brand and Wissen, 2021), capitalism naturalizes itself and nature becomes a business, a mixture of living and dead labour waiting to be exploited. Within this framework, as the context of the delta shows, the intensification of the main guidelines of agricultural development and the process of irreversible modification of territories and their biodiversity have gone hand in hand with the intensification of marginalization dynamics brought about by colonization. These dynamics imply processes of redefinition of social relations linked to land and territories, where important social and ecological struggles have been and are still being fought.

The latter, and the local conflicts from which they arise, illustrate how, for a wide range of populations, the promise of future inclusion through growth, more prosperity and the improvement of the quality of life is destined not so much to become a broken assumption as to cease to be formulated at all. In its place, the inevitability of development is presented as a process of rationalizing and improving the world, in the name of a necessarily global response to planetary crises. However, the narratives of environmental justice that emerge from local contexts, embodied in subjects, practices and relations to territories, offer different ways of thinking about current problems and their solutions. They invite a re-reading of the history of development by creating space for alternative representations that allow for pathways of reconnection capable of producing concrete effects.

It is against this background that struggles and contexts that are often very distant from each other find themselves connected in a global dialogue, bringing forward common, yet ecologically situated reflections, producing not only new knowledge, but also showing how the latter is articulated within the multiple histories that run through modernity as lines of fracture. These make it impossible to 'reduce modernity to capitalism' (Mezzadra, 2011, p 158) despite the latter's constitutive role, and produce points of friction and disconnection that seem to emerge strongly today in the context of socio-ecological struggles over territory and reproduction.

Mobilized against the expropriation of their pasture lands, local pastoralists are now committed to fighting back against green capitalism and the expansion of agrarian extractivism. Their struggle also testifies to the difficult transition faced by pastoralists across the Sahel. As previously said, access to land is undoubtedly crucial for the future sustainability of pastoral activities. However, local land demands cannot be disconnected from a socio-ecological vision of development, which is radically opposed to the narratives of modernization that have framed pastoralist political ecologies since the era of colonization. If we pay attention to the discourses at the local level, it becomes evident that, contrary to the dominant narratives, pastoralists are actually fighting for what we can define as radical and future-oriented transformations. They are promoting a vision of transition that breaks with the developmental and colonial legacy towards more equitable and sustainable models of coexistence between agriculture and pastoralism.

While the effectiveness of green capitalism solutions in matching social and environmental sustainability is seriously under question, numerous experiments are already under way in the Sahel (Scoones and Toulmin, 2021). However, local needs cannot be grasped without taking into account the desire of many herders to preserve the social and environmental sustainability of a practice whose importance stems from cultural, economic and ecological reasons that cannot be separated from one another. The land-grabbing phenomenon has put the urgency of pastoralist claims back at the centre of the political arena. This makes it important to understand how these are not only about resisting the processes of dispossession and marginalization, but also about supporting alternative narratives and visions, capable of giving value to the other developmental paths that have existed alongside colonial modernity.

Notes

Introduction

1 This figure was later revised downwards by the Food and Agriculture Organization in a new statistical calculation that raised some criticism. For an analysis on this topic, see Lappé et al (2013).

2 The idea of the 'global South' emerged in the 1970s as a counterpoint to that of the Third World – at a time when global power relations were different from those of today – and established itself as a 'geo-political' rather than merely geographical concept. Today, the notion of the global South is at the centre of a lively debate, owing to the altered circumstances of global capitalism, and since it refers to an extremely heterogeneous set of countries with different economic and socio-economic indicators and with distinct relations with respect to the colonial model and economy (especially China), it nevertheless has the merit of not indexing the different national experiences on a time scale based on economic and cultural development phases, according to a historicist paradigm that has already been proved wrong in its conceptual and practical axioms (on this final point see, for instance, Chakrabarty, 2000, pp 27–115).

3 Statement by F.S., village of Y., April 2015.

4 The first edition of the book (2021) takes place at the same time as the start of this debate, so this section has been updated for the new English-language edition of the book.

5 The field research took place between 2013 and 2015, with a duration of six months, followed by both remote and in person interviews and updates up to the present day.

6 The idea of commodity frontiers aims to explain how specific local contexts are shaped and how, in turn, they shape the expansion of the accumulation process involving both an international division of labour and the inclusion of ever new resources into the production process. Commodity frontiers are both expansive and intensive, external and internal: they range from the creation of new sites for the extraction of fossil fuels and minerals to the expansion of plantations and the biological exploitation of bodies, genes and cells. They are also sites of struggles, where the production of knowledge, norms and nature that can shape human ecology and political structures at various levels and geographical scales are bitterly contested .

7 For a discussion on the idea of development as a politically contested space influencing the form that capitalism takes in postcolonial context, rather than the depoliticized version of the capitalist economic project, see Sanyal (2007).

Chapter 1

1 Actually, the total amount of land obtained by the Senhuile-Senethanol consortium in Senegal might be greater and also include an additional 5,000 hectares granted in the community of Fass Ngom, also located in the Senegal delta, according to interviews conducted in October 2014 with members of the rural community. However, it was

not possible to confirm the current status of the land, nor to know the details of the concession. For a discussion of Senhuile concessions in Senegal, see also Bagnoli et al (2015, p 33) and Figure 3.1.

2 According to the 1964 Land Law, *Loi sur le Domaine National*, there are three categories of land in Senegal: state land (both public and private); national land; and private land held by individuals with registered titles. The 'national domain', which covers most of the country's land, and 95 per cent of the territory at the time of its enactment, is further divided into: *zones urbaines*, *zones de terroirs*, *zones classées* and *zones pionnières*. The former correspond to municipal territories, with an urban vocation or predisposed to urban expansion, and also include agricultural-urban lands. The *zones de terroirs* indicate rural areas consisting of land used for family farming and livestock breeding. Allocation by the rural community is conditional on the ability of the grantee to 'put to productive use' (*mise en valeur*) such areas as well as on residence, although the latter provision tends to be less observed. The third category, *zones classées*, includes forests and nature reserves, currently governed by the Code Forestier and placed under the protection of the rural community. These areas meet a need for environmental conservation but are also intended as a temporary reserve to be preserved for future use and are therefore often subject to reclassification in order to be developed. The *zones pionnières*, a kind of reserve territory with respect to previous ones, are meant to accommodate major development and planning programmes (particularly agricultural) and the law describes them as unused or new land.

3 Since 2013, with the enactment of Law No. 2013-10 of 28 December, rural communities have been transformed into municipalities as part of the decentralization reforms under Act III.

4 For a discussion of the corporate structure and identity of shareholders, see https://www.grain.org/article/entries/4815-who-is-behind-senhuile-senethanol [accessed 30 September 2020].

5 Decree no. 2012-366, *Portant déclassement partiel de la réserve spéciale de Ndiaël* and Decree no. 2012-367, *Portant affectation d'une assiette foncière au projet agro-industriel Senhuile-Senethanol*, République du Sénégal, Dakar, 20 March 2012.

6 Partly because of the fascination that nomadic-pastoral populations have exercised in many researchers, colonial and otherwise, Africanist literature has dealt extensively with the Fulanis. Between the second half of the 19th century and the first half of the 20th century, the origin of the Fulanis was the subject of a long dispute marked by various theses, and subsequent denials, that assumed an Indo-European, Caucasian genesis, and direct descent from the inhabitants of Ancient Egypt. Attempts to prove a Middle Eastern and non-African origin of these populations have eventually been connected to the prejudice of colonial science whereby the state-military organizations of the Fulɓe empires were thought to be too advanced for African populations and the Fulanis were defined as 'almost white' and placed at the top of the racial hierarchy (on this, see Williams, 1988). More recently, the autonomy of the Fulani identity, with respect to African identities as a whole, has been questioned and ascribed to a colonially prejudiced 'anthropological reason' incapable of thinking of the other except through classifications and mappings that nevertheless respond to an exogenous need to 'bring order' (Amselle, 1998). In opposition to the idea of multiculturalism and cultural relativism – and formulating a political critique of colonial anthropology and its legacies in the contemporary world – Amselle supports the idea of an African society structured as an identity *continuum*, where the boundary lines of otherness – and therefore of identity – are mobile and always relational, rather than the product of distinct and original foundational paths. Similarly, the line separating the individual from other ethnic categories is liable to transitions, absorption and further separation, thus constituting a porous barrier between multiple identities. According

to Amselle, the Fulani identity itself does not have an autonomous origin but is rather rooted 'in a primary multi-ethnic situation that would include, for example, those people speaking the related languages of Fulani, Serer, Wolof, Mandingo or the Volta languages. A primary multiethnic situation that would have given rise to the different ethnic identities in the forms eventually fixed by colonial thought' (Amselle, 1998, p 45, English translation). In the light of these considerations, it is then appropriate to point out that this text, when naming the Fulani identities, takes an emic point of view, that is, it reports the forms of self-representation collected in ethnographic fieldwork. While this does not contradict the French anthropologist's thesis on the mobility of ethnic identities, it does not preclude that the perceived identity might have asserted itself by leveraging aspects such as language, customs and traditions, but also and above all socio-political events. On this last point, one could argue that Amselle's thesis is congruent with the idea of marginality as defined in this book, where the French anthropologist states that '[a]s historical beings, the Fulani result from a double process of absorption and elimination, or of coming together and expulsion, which encapsulates a large part of West African history' and that, therefore, 'what appears … as a distinct Fulani entity is in reality the result of a continual modification of political formations and an evolution of the relations of forces between Islam and "paganism"' (Amselle, 1998, pp 46 and 49, English translation).

7 Decree no. 65-053, *Portant classement des réserves partielles de faune du Boundoum et de Djeuse avec classement compensateur de la réserve spéciale de faune du N'Diael*, République du Sénégal, Dakar, 1965.

8 Part of this area is now home to the Djoudj national bird sanctuary.

9 This is, however, mentioned in a few studies such as that of Cissokho (1998, p 66).

10 The Ramsar project also has a mission to '[c]onserve and rationally use wetlands through local, regional and national actions and international cooperation as a contribution to achieving sustainable development worldwide'. In the report of the Ramsar mission of 7 December 1988 in Senegal, the commission in charge of the visit to the area was composed, among others, of Patrick Triplet, a member of the CIC, and Christian Virmaud of the Association de Chasse et Tir du Sénégal, which in turn represented several local associations interested in the development of hunting tourism and ornithological observation in the Ndiaël cuvette and in the Trois Marigots area. The report can be consulted at http://www.ramsar.org/fr/a-propos/la-convention-de-ramsar-et-sa-mission [accessed 30 October 2020].

11 Founded in 1960, the Institut de Recherches Agronomiques Tropicales et des Cultures Vivrières (IRAT; Institute for Research on Tropical Agronomics and Food Crops) is a French institute specializing in agronomic research that originally welcomed many researchers formerly linked to the Ministry of Colonies.

12 For a similar analysis, see Ciavolella (2010, chapter 1 [especially 1.2]).

13 The delta region, except for the Atlantic Ocean, knows no precise administrative boundaries and also extends to the Mauritanian shore. According to certain scholars, 'delta' also means the area on the eastern shore of Lake Guiers. For the purposes of this book, we only refer to the Senegalese part to the left of the lake, as also defined in Tourrand (2000).

14 Between 200 mm per year in the north and 300 mm in the south.

15 Which was later renamed Société nationale d'aménagement et d'exploitation des terres du delta du fleuve Sénégal et des vallées du fleuve Sénégal et de la Falémé [National Company for the Development and Exploitation of the Lands of the Senegal River Delta and the Valleys of the Senegal and Falémé Rivers].

16 See note no 2 in this chapter.

17 Calculated on the basis of data from Tourrand (2000).

18 For Senegal and the Vallée, see Santoir (1977).

19 For a critical review of the concept of poverty applied to pastoralism, see Duteurtre and Faye (2009, pp 9–16).

20 Decree no. 80-268, *Portant organisation des parcours du bétail et fixant les conditions d'utilisation des pâturages*, République du Sénégal, Dakar, 10 March 1980.

21 Gouvernement du sénégal, *Nouvelle Initiative sectorielle pour le développement de l'élevage*, République du Sénégal, Dakar, October 2004, p 6.

Chapter 2

1 For a recent update on the debate, see Péclard et al (2020).

2 Available at http://www.fao.org/worldfoodsituation/foodpricesindex/en/ [accessed 30 September 2020].

3 FAO, *Food Outlook December 2009*, Global Market Analysis, Rome 2009. Available at http://www.fao.org/3/ak341e/ak341e00.htm [accessed 30 October 2020].

4 FAO, *Food Outlook December 2009*, Global Market Analysis, Rome 2009. Available at http://www.fao.org/3/ak341e/ak341e00.htm [accessed 30 October 2020].

5 As early as the early 2000s, several internal and independent reports had already negatively commented on the performance of the main global institutions dealing with agricultural and food policies, including the Food and Agriculture Organization and the Consultative Group on International Agricultural Research. The most notable of these reports is perhaps the one commissioned by the World Bank in 2007, which recognized the failure of structural adjustment policies and considered the development programmes conducted in Africa since 1990 to be ineffective in addressing agricultural sector issues (World Bank, 2007b).

6 These could, in turn, refer to European agricultural experiences, embodied in the Common Agricultural Policy, and those of Maoist China (the Great Leap Forward policy inaugurated by Mao Zedong in 1958), both of which represented contemporary interpretations of agricultural policies based on self-sufficiency, protectionism and interventionism.

7 See the Via Campesina website, which also provides further insights into the concept of food sovereignty: https://viacampesina.org/en/food-sovereignty/ [accessed 30 October 2020].

8 While the role of the Reagan and Thatcher governments in financial deregulation and the adoption of neoliberal policies is fairly well known, that of their transalpine neighbours has received less attention. Yet, in a way, the 'Paris Consensus' was a forerunner of the 'Washington Consensus'. On this topic, see Abdelal (2005).

9 On the impacts of agro-industry, see, for instance, Horrigan et al (2002).

10 The Environment, Food and Rural Affairs Committee is a government body appointed by the House of Commons and its role is to examine the expenditure, administration and policy of the Department for Environment, Food and Rural Affairs and its associated bodies.

11 Together with Monsanto, Syngenta, Dow AgroSciences, DuPont, Bayer, and BASF, Cargill was part of the so-called Big Six, that is, the six agro-food companies that controlled 70 per cent of the market in 2007, producing about three-quarters of the total pesticides on the world market. After the Big Six, come the Big Eight, covering 92 per cent of the global food market (see Shand, 2014).

Chapter 3

1 After obtaining self-government within the framework of the French Community in 1958, Senegal became part of the Mali Federation on 20 June 1960, only to abandon it two months later and proclaim itself an autonomous republic with Léopold Sédar Senghor as its president.

2 In addition to Léopold Sédar Senghor in Senegal, other leading theorists of African socialism include Julius Nyerere (first president of Tanzania), Modibo Keïta (first president of Mali) and Kwame Nkrumah (prime minister of Ghana).

3 In 1981, the publication of the Berg Report by the World Bank marked a shift in economic development theories from a more interventionist approach in which the government was understood as a key actor in the development process to a free-market approach based on deregulation, reliance on the private sector and downsizing of the role of the state. Based on this report, the Structural Adjustment Programmes were designed with the aim of reducing the fiscal imbalances of debtor countries and promoting their economic growth. The programmes consist of ten political-economic directives, often referred to as the Washington Consensus, that states are required to respect and implement in order to access development funding from the International Monetary Fund and the World Bank.

4 The CFA franc (originally from Colonies Françaises d'Afrique, later to become the acronym for Communauté financière d'Afrique) is the common currency of the 14 states of French-speaking Africa and is divided into two separate currencies: the franc of the West Africa Economic and Monetary Union and of the Central African Economic and Monetary Community and the Comoros. Since 1945, with the approval of the Bretton-Woods Agreements, the value of this currency has been indexed to the French currency and, since 1999, to the euro, which implies a fixed exchange rate and the impossibility for African states to decide their own financial and monetary policy. The convertibility of the CFA franc is guaranteed by the French Treasury whose coffers contain 50 per cent of the currency reserves of the countries of the monetary zone in CFA francs and 65 per cent of the reserves of the Comorian franc. For a critical history of the mechanism, see Pigeaud and Sylla (2018).

5 Reconfirmed in office in 2007, A. Wade ended his second term in 2012 in a climate of strong protest also due to corruption scandals involving his administration. It is worth mentioning the presence of a youth movement in the opponents' ranks, united under the slogan 'Y'en a Marre' ('We are fed up'), that organized street protests throughout 2011 and 2012. The successor to A. Wade, who is still in office, is Macky Sall, prime minister at the time of the Wade government and special advisor to the President of the Republic from 2000 to 2001 as well as Minister of Mines, Energy and Hydraulics (May 2001–August 2003) and Minister of the Interior (August 2003–April 2004). He broke away from A. Wade and founded his own party, the Alliance pour la Republique, with which he stood in the February 2012 elections and won in the second round runoff.

6 République du Sénégal, *Programme spécial biocarburants 2007/2012*, Dakar, July 2007.

7 Decree no. 2006-1336, *Portant création, organisation et fonctionnement de l'Agence nationale Retour Vers l'Agriculture (REVA)*, République du Sénégal, Dakar, 29 November 2006.

8 For a perspective on the notion of flexibility associated with these plants, see Borras et al (2016).

9 Information also cited in Sensi (2012).

10 The legislative texts merely discriminate positively for sustainable biomass by reserving higher incentives for it. However, if one tries to understand what the definition of sustainability refers to, one sees that the Italian legislation refers to European Directive 2009/28/EC in which there is no operational definition.

11 See, for example, Brambilla (2005).

12 See, for example, the settlement at the bottom left of Figure 3.2.

13 See Figure 3.1.

14 Decree no. 2012-366, *Portant déclassement partiel de la réserve spéciale de Ndiaël* and Decree no. 2012-367, *Portant affectation d'une assiette foncière au projet agro-industriel Senhuile-Senethanol*, République du Sénégal, Dakar, 20 March 2012.

15 Decree no. 2012-366, *Portant déclassement partiel de la réserve spéciale de Ndiaël* and Decree no. 2012-367, *Portant affectation d'une assiette foncière au projet agro-industriel Senhuile-Senethanol*, République du Sénégal, Dakar, 20 March 2012.

16 This decision was probably suggested to the company by the local technical authorities as it repeats the practice used by SAED to organize the space between the villages and their fields.

17 Decree no. 2012-448, *Abrogeant le décret 2012-366 du 20 Mars 2012 portant déclassement partiel de la réserve spéciale de Ndiaël et le décret 2012-317 du 20 Mars 2012 portant affectation d'une assiette foncière au projet agro-industriel Senhuile-Senethanol*, République du Sénégal, Dakar, 12 April 2012.

18 Decree no. 2012-822, *Abrogeant le décret 2012-448 du 12 avril 2012 portant abrogation du décret 2012-366 du 20 Mars 2012 portant déclassement partiel de la réserve spéciale de Ndiaël et le décret 2012-317 du 20 Mars 2012 portant affectation d'une assiette foncière au projet agro-industriel Senhuile-Senethanol*, République du Sénégal, Dakar, 6 August 2012.

19 See the company's presentation of its history on its website at https://vegetableoil.tampieri.com/it/chi_siamo [accessed 30 September 2020].

20 For a detailed analysis of the impact study and its critical issues, see Benegiamo and Cirillo (2014).

21 The approximate figure is the result of a field survey by GPS analysis carried out in April 2014.

22 The company later declared that it had planted a total of 28,752 trees belonging to the *Acacias Meliféra* and *Leucaena* family, for an investment of 12,500,000 CFA (about 18,000 euros). However, it does not specify whether these trees correspond in number, location and species to those it had previously eradicated. Acacias are highly susceptible to pest and their introduction into an ecosystem must be done with extreme caution. The same applies to the *Leucaena*, which in addition to not being a native species is intolerant of high salinity soils such as those found in the Ndiaël Reserve. The company justified its actions by stating that it wanted to contribute to environmental preservation and sustainable development. Actually, these reforestation activities, rather than environmental compensation, were more likely intended to create a wind barrier to protect the plantations.

23 Law no. 2001-01 of 12 April 2001, *Portant code de l'environnement*, in particular, Article 48, and Annex 1. See also Article 38 of Decree no. 2001-282, *Portant application du code de l'environnement*, Government of Senegal, Dakar, 12 April 2001 and the relevant ministerial orders (nos. 9468 and 9469). Order no. 9468 specifies that persons affected by the study must be duly informed and are authorized to provide their comments verbally or in writing, and at different stages of processing.

Chapter 4

1 Letter to the Governor of the Saint-Louis Region signed by Le Collectif des 37 villages du Ndiaël, Kadd Ndeff, le 10 septembre 2012, unpublished document provided by the drafters.

2 Letter to the Governor of the Saint-Louis Region signed by Le Collectif des 37 villages du Ndiaël, Kadd Ndeff, le 10 septembre 2012, unpublished document provided by the drafters.

3 It goes without saying that there is a discrepancy between the formality and rigour with which the consultation process is documented by the population and the lack of transparency in the negotiations between the company and the national institutions.

4 *Conclusions de la rencontre des habitants concernés par le projet du Ndiaël*, Rosso Béthio, 8 August 2012, unpublished document provided by the drafters.

5 Demonstration, Ndiaël, 21 January 2014, transcript from the video of the demonstration published by the news site Ndarinfo.com and available at https://www.youtube.com/watch?v=bAaSn-UE5uc [accessed 30 September 2020].

6 Statement by S.S., village of Y., November 2014.
7 For a discussion on this term, see Ciavolella (2010).
8 Statement by A.S., village of J., March 2014.
9 Statement by S.S., village of Y., November 2014.
10 For a detailed analysis of the company's statements, see Bagnoli et al (2015).
11 This association, which also deals with the social aspects of the other enterprises of Senhuile's director, is the local division of an international non-governmental organization, which is also financed by Elton John through his concerts. See Benegiamo and Cirillo (2014).
12 The petition is available at https://www.grain.org/article/entries/4900-despaysans-et-eleveurs-senegalais-exigent-que-la-multinationale-senhuile-sa-quitte-leurs-terres [accessed 13 September 2020].
13 Interview with D.T., Dakar, 30 April 2014.
14 See, for example, the statements and video interview published on the news site Ndarinfo.com. Available at https://www.ndarinfo.com/AGROBUSINESS-SEN-HUILE-Le-DG-satisfait-des-performances-agricoles-de-sa-societe-video_a12555.html [accessed 30 September 2020].
15 See also the interview published by the news site Senenews. Available at https://www.senenews.com/actualites/economie/itw-du-week-end-massimo-castellucci-dg-de-senhuile-le-secteur-prive-en-afrique-peut-jouer-un-role-extremement-important-pour-le-developpement-du-continent_122044.html [accessed 30 September 2020].
16 https://www.senenews.com/actualites/economie/itw-du-week-end-massimo-castellucci-dg-de-senhuile-le-secteur-prive-en-afrique-peut-jouer-un-role-extremement-important-pour-le-developpement-du-continent_122044.html [accessed 30 September 2020].
17 The United Nations (2011) has tried to articulate the idea of accountability by combining the three principles of 'Protect, Respect and Remedy', but this remains limited to serious violations of universal human rights, and little is said about the indirect and socio-economic or inequality impacts of business activities.
18 Communauté Rurale de Ngnith, *Protocole d'accord entre Senhuile SA et le Collectif des Villages riverains du Projet*, January 2014, and Communauté Rurale de Ronkh, *Protocole d'accord entre Senhuile SA et le Collectif des Villages riverains du Projet*, January 2014. Unpublished documents, available online at Senuhile.com, which is no longer accessible.
19 See what was stated in the video published on the Ndarinfo news site, http://www.ndarinfo.com/VIDEO-NGNITH-lespopulations-louent-les-actions-sociales-de-SEN-HUILE_a12556.html [accessed 30 September 2020].
20 In fact, the company benefits from a concession from the government which, if confirmed by the absence of an emphyteusis contract, does not give it full ownership rights but is limited to usufruct.
21 Interview with S.K., village of K.D., November 2014.
22 Interview with A.K., village of K.D., February 2014.
23 Interview with A.K., village of K.D., February 2014.
24 Statement by S.S., village of J., October 2014.

Conclusion

1 Available at http://www.pdidas.org/index.php/fr/ [accessed 30 September 2020].

References

Abdelal, R. (2005) 'Le Consensus de Paris et les règles de la finance mondiale', *Critique Internationale*, 28(3), 87–115. doi: 10.3917/crii.028.0087

Acosta, A. (2013) 'Extractivism and Neoextractivism: Two Sides of the Same Curse', in Lang, M. and Mokrani, D. (eds) *Beyond Development: Alternative Visions from Latin America*. Amsterdam/Quito: Transnational Institute/RosaLuxemburg Foundation, pp 61–86.

Akinocho, A. (2014) 'Koffi Annan appelle à une transformation de l'agriculture africaine', *Agence EcoFin*. Available at: http://www.agenceecofin.com/gestion-publique/0108-21945-koffi-annan-appelle-a-une-transformation-de-l-agriculture-africaine [Accessed 30 September 2020].

Akram-Lodhi, A.H. (2021) 'The Ties That Bind? Agroecology and the Agrarian Question in the Twenty-First Century', *Journal of Peasant Studies*, 48(4), 687–714. doi: 10.1080/03066150.2021.1923010

Alliegro, E.V. (2012) *Il Totem Nero: Petrolio, Sviluppo e Conflitti in Basilicata*. Rome: CISU.

Alonso-Fradejas, A. (2015) 'Anything but a Story Foretold: Multiple Politics of Resistance to the Agrarian Extractivist Project in Guatemala', *Journal of Peasant Studies*, 42(3–4), 489–515. doi: 10.1080/03066150.2015.1013468

Amanor, K.S. (2012) 'Global Resource Grabs, Agribusiness Concentration and the Smallholder: Two West African Case Studies', *The Journal of Peasant Studies*, 39(3–4), 731–749. doi: 10.1080/03066150.2012.676543

Amselle, J.-L. (1998) *Mestizo Logics: Anthropology of Identity in Africa and Elsewhere*. Stanford: Stanford University Press.

Anseeuw, W., Boche, M., Breu, T., Giger, M., Lay, J., Messerli, P., et al (2012) *Transnational Land Deals for Agriculture in the Global South: Analytical Report Based on the Land Matrix Database*. Bern/Montpellier/Hamburg: CDE/CIRAD/GIG.

Antil, R. (2010) *Les 'émeutes de la faim' au Sénégal. Une puissance révélatrice d'une défaillance de gouvernance*. Paris: IFRI.

Argo, F. (1976) 'Monumenti della Valle del Fiume Senegal'. *Africa: Rivista trimestrale di studi e documentazione dell'Istituto italiano per l'Africa e l'Oriente*, 31(4), 569–585.

Armiero, M., Andritsos, T., Barca, S., Brás, R., Cauyela, S.R., Dedeoğlu, Ç., et al (2019) 'Toxic Bios: Toxic Autobiographies – a Public Environmental Humanities Project', *Environmental Justice*, 12(1), 7–11. doi: 10.1089/env.2018.0019

Audru, J. (1996) *Etude des pâturages naturels et des problèmes pastoraux dans le Delta du fleuve Sénégal.* Tome 1: description du milieu, Tome 2: politique de l'élevage (Étude agrostologique No. 15). Maisons-Alfort: Institut d'élevage et de médecine vétérinaire des pays tropicaux.

Ba, B. (2008) *Agriculture et sécurité alimentaire au Sénégal.* Paris: L'Harmattan.

Baglioni, E. (2015) 'Straddling Contract and Estate Farming: Accumulation Strategies of Senegalese Horticultural Exporters', *Journal of Agrarian Change*, 15(1), 17–42. doi: 10.1111/joac.12032

Baglioni, E. and Gibbon, P. (2013) 'Land Grabbing, Large- and Small-scale Farming: What Can Evidence and Policy from 20th Century Africa Contribute to the Debate?', *Third World Quarterly*, 34(9), 1558–1581. http://www.jstor.org/stable/24522198

Bagnoli, L., Benegiamo, M. and Cirillo, D. (2015) *Senegal, come si accaparra la terra.* Rome: RE:COMMON.

Barca, S. (2020) *Forces of Reproduction: Notes for a Counter-hegemonic Anthropocene.* Cambridge: Cambridge University Press.

Barry, B. (2014) *Le royaume du Waalo: le Sénégal avant la conquête.* Paris: Karthala.

Battistoni, A. (2017) 'Bringing in the Work of Nature: From Natural Capital to Hybrid Labor', *Political Theory*, 45(1), 5–31. https://www.jstor.org/stable/44509301

Bayart, J.F. (2006) *L'État en Afrique: La Politique du Ventre.* Paris: Fayard.

Beck, U. (1992) *Risk Society: Towards a New Modernity.* London: SAGE.

Beier, U. (ed) (1966) *The Origin of Life and Death: African Creation Myths.* Nairobi: East African Publishers.

Benegiamo, M. (2020) 'Extractivism, Exclusion and Conflicts in Senegal's Agro-industrial Transformation', *Review of African Political Economy*, 47(166), 522–544. doi:10.1080/03056244.2020.1794661

Benegiamo, M. (2021) 'Exploring Accumulation in the New Green Revolution for Africa: Ecological Crisis, Agrarian Development and Bio-Capitalism', in Benquet, M. and Bourgeron, T. (eds) *Accumulating Capital Today.* London: Routledge, pp 61–74. doi: 10.4324/9781003089513

Benegiamo, M. (2022) 'A "Green Economy" Failure? Italian Investors in Senegal Between Green Grabbing and Development Promises', *Sociologia Urbana e Rurale*, 129, 30–51. doi: 10.3280/SUR2022-129002

Benegiamo, M. and Cirillo, D. (2014) *No Land, No Future: A Community's Struggle to Reclaim their Land.* Johannesburg: ActionAid International.

Benegiamo, M. and Cirillo, D. (2016) 'Agroindustria e pastorizia nel Delta del fiume Senegal. Dai margini ai limiti dello sviluppo', in Bin, S., Donadelli, G., Quatrida, D. and Visentin, F. (eds) *Labor Limites. Riconoscere, vivere e riprogettare i limiti*. Milano: Franco Angeli, pp 116–129. Available at: https://ojs.francoangeli.it/_omp/index.php/oa/catalog/book/165 [Accessed 30 October 2020].

Bonnet, B. and Hérault, D. (2011) 'Governance of Pastoral Tenure and Climate Change in the Sahel: Reinforce Capacities of Actors to Secure Mobility and Fair Access to Pastoral Resources', *Land Tenure Journal*, 2, 157–187, FAO-2011. Available at: https://openknowledge.fao.org/server/api/core/bitstreams/1477d3f9-716e-4762-9bca-17a1c45c8171/content [Accessed 30 October 2020].

Borras Jr., S.M., Franco, J.C., Isakson, S.R., Levidow, L. and Vervest, P. (2016) 'The Rise of Flex Crops and Commodities: Implications for Research', *The Journal of Peasant Studies*, 43(1), 93–115. doi:10.1080/03066150.2015.1036417

Bourguignon, D. (2015) *EU Biofuels Policy: Dealing with Indirect Land Use Change*. Policy Briefing, European Parliament Think Tank. Available at: https://www.europarl.europa.eu/RegData/etudes/BRIE/2015/545726/EPRS_BRI(2015)545726_REV1_EN.pdf [Accessed 30 September 2020].

Boyd, W., Scott Prudham, W. and Schurman, R.A. (2011) 'Industrial Dynamics and the Problem of Nature', *Society & Natural Resources*, 14(7), 555–570. doi: 10.1080/08941920120686

Brambilla, C. (2005) 'Confini, cartografia e identità: l'esempio della frontiera coloniale tra Ghana e Togo', *Bollettino dell'Associazione Italiana di Cartografia*, 123-124-125, 285–296.

Brand, U. and Wissen, M. (2021) *The Imperial Mode of Living: Everyday Life and the Ecological Crisis of Capitalism*. London: Verso Books.

Breedveld, A. and De Bruijn, M. (1996) 'L'image des Fulbe: Analyse critique de la construction du concept de pulaaku', *Cahiers d'Études Africaines*, 36(144), 791–821.

Bruna, N. (2023) *The Rise of Green Extractivism: Extractivism, Rural Livelihoods and Accumulation in a Climate-smart World*. Oxon-New York: Routledge.

Bullard, R.D. (2001) 'Environmental Justice in the 21st Century: Race Still Matters', *Phylon (1960–)*, 49(3/4), 151–171. doi: 10.2307/3132626

Büscher, B. (2012) 'The Political Economy of Africa's Natural Resources and the "Great Financial Crisis"', *Tijdschrift voor Economische en Sociale Geografie*, 103(2), 136–149. doi: 10.1111/j.1467-9663.2012.00708.x

Bush, R. (2009) 'Food Riots: Poverty, Power and Protest', *Journal of Agrarian Change*, 10, 119–129. doi: 10.1111/j.1471-0366.2009.00253.x

Calzolari, T. (2011) 'Tampieri dopo Report: "Se devo sentir parlare male, non farò più niente"', *RavennaToday*. Available at: https://www.ravennatoday.it/cronaca/tampieri-faenza-intervista-giovanni-tampieri-su-puntata-report.html [Accessed 30 September 2020].

Carbone, G., Bruno, G.P., Calchi Novati, G. and Montanini, M. (2013) *Scommettere sull'Africa Emergente: Opportunità e Scenari della Presenza Italiana nell'Africa Subsahariana*. Milan: ISPI.

Carrosio, G. (2011) *I Biocarburanti: Globalizzazione e Politiche Territoriali*. Rome: Carocci.

Castañeda, D. (2005) 'Les organisations d'éleveurs et de pasteurs au Sénégal, approche socio-politique', *Réflexions et Perspectives*, 6(1), ISRA, Dakar. Available at: https://www.bameinfopol.info/IMG/pdf/RP_Vol.6_n.1.pdf [Accessed 30 September 2020].

Cesaro, J.D., Magrin, G. and Ninot, O. (2010) *Atlas de l'élevage au Sénégal: commerces et territoires*. Paris: PRODIG.

CFS (Committee on World Food Security) (2012) *Coming to Terms with Terminology: Food Security, Nutrition Security, Food Security and Nutrition, Food and Nutrition Security*. Proceedings of the 39th session of the Committee on World Food Security. Available at: http://www.fao.org/3/MD776E/MD776E.pdf [Accessed 30 October 2020].

Chagnon, C.W., Durante, F., Barry, K., Gills, S.E., Hagolani-Albov, S., Hokkanen, S., et al (2022) 'From Extractivism to Global Extractivism: The Evolution of an Organizing Concept', *The Journal of Peasant Studies*, 49(4), 760–792. doi:10.1080/03066150.2022.2069015

Chakrabarty, D. (2000) *Provincializing Europe: Postcolonial Thought and Historical Difference*. Princeton: Princeton University Press.

Chiaroni, D., Frattini, F. and Terruzzi, R. (2011) *Il business delle biomasse e dei bio- carburanti nel sistema industriale italiano*, Biomass Energy Report, Collana Quaderni AIP. Milan: Politecnico di Milano.

Ciavolella, R. (2010) *Les Peuls et l'état en Mauritanie. une anthropologie des marges*. Paris: Karthala.

Cissokho, A. (1998) 'Localisation, accessibilité des zones de pâturages et des points d'eau pastoraux. Conditions de développement d'un élevage pastoral dans le delta du Fleuve Sénégal', Mémoire de maîtrise AA. 1997–1998, Université Gaston Berger, Saint Louis.

Colin de Verdière, P. (1995) *Les conséquences de la sédentarisation de l'élevage au Sahel. Étude comparée de trois systèmes agropastoraux dans la région de Filingué (Niger)*. Thèse de doctorat, Institut national agronomique Paris-Grignon, Paris.

Comité Français pour la Solidarité Internationale (CSI) (2013) *Le Projet Jatropha de Nuove Iniziative Industriali en République de Guinée*. Comité Français pour la Solidarité Internationale. Available at: https://www.coordinationsud.org/wp-content/uploads/767_guinee_energie_cfsi-sosfaim-copagen.pdf [Accessed 30 September 2020].

Cooper, M.E. (2008) *Life as Surplus: Biotechnology and Capitalism in the Neoliberal Era.* Seattle: University of Washington Press.

Copans, J. (1980) *Les Marabouts de l'Arachide: La Confrérie Mouride et les Paysans du Sénégal.* Paris: L'Harmattan.

Damgé, M. (2013) 'Les profits des négociants de matières premières dépassent ceux des banques', *Le Monde.fr.* Available at: https://www.lemonde.fr/economie/article/2013/04/16/les-profits-des-negociants-de-matieres-premieres-depassent-ceux-des-banques_3160114_3234.html [Accessed 30 September 2020].

Davis, M. (2006) *Planet of Slums.* London: Verso Books.

De Bakker, F.G.A. and Den Hond, F. (2008) 'Introducing the Politics of Stakeholder Influence: A Review Essay', *Business & Society*, 47, 8–20. doi:10.1177/0007650307306637

Deininger, K. and Byerlee, D. (2011) *Rising Global Interest in Farmland: Agriculture and Rural Development.* Washington, DC: World Bank.

Derex, J.M. (2001) 'Pour une histoire des zones humides en France (XVIIe-XIXe siècle)', *Histoire et Sociétés Rurales*, 15(1), 11–36.

Diagne, P.S. (1974) *Le delta du fleuve Sénégal: problèmes de développement.* Thèse de 3eme cycle, Université de Paris I, Paris.

Dupire, M. (1962) *Peuls nomades: étude descriptive des Woddaabé du Sahel nigérien.* Paris: Karthala.

Duteurtre, G. and Faye, B. (eds) (2009) *L'élevage, richesse des pauvres: Stratégies d'éleveurs et organisations sociales face aux risques dans les pays du Sud.* Versailles: Éditions Quæ.

DW (2008) 'Merkel to G8: Food Crisis is Global Security Risk', *Deutsche Welle*, 5 July. Available at: https://p.dw.com/p/EWoh [Accessed 30 September 2020].

Economic Community of West African States (ECOWAS) (2008) *Élevage et marché régional au Sahel et en Afrique de l'Ouest.* Paris: CSAO/OCDE.

Edelman, M., Oya, C. and Borras Jr., S.M. (2013) 'Global Land Grabs: Historical Processes, Theoretical and Methodological Implications and Current Trajectories', *Third World Quarterly*, 34(9), 1517–1531. doi:10.1080/01436597.2013.850190

Estève, C. (2006) 'La chasse au gibier d'eau en France au 19e siècle', *Ruralia*, 18/19. http://journals.openedition.org/ruralia/1161

EuropAfrica (2011) *Biofueling Injustice?* Available at: https://www.fian.be/IMG/pdf/biofueling_injustice_complete_.pdf [Accessed 30 September 2020].

Fairbairn, M. (2014) '"Like Gold with Yield": Evolving Intersections between Farmland and Finance', *Journal of Peasant Studies*, 41(5), 777–795. doi: 10.1080/03066150.2013.873977

Fairhead, J., Leach, M. and Scoones, I. (2012) 'Green Grabbing: A New Appropriation of Nature?', *The Journal of Peasant Studies*, 39(2), 237–261. doi: 10.1080/03066150.2012.671770

Fanon, F. (2005) *The Wretched of the Earth*. New York: Grove Press.
FAO (Food and Agriculture Organization) (1983) *World Food Security: A Reappraisal of the Concepts and Approaches* (Director General's Report). Rome: FAO.
FAO (1996) *Rome Declaration on World Food Security and World Food Summit Plan of Action*. Rome: FAO.
FAO (2008a) *The State of Food Insecurity in the World 2008: High Food Prices and Food Security. Threats and Opportunities*. Rome: FAO.
FAO (2008b) *High-Level Conference on World Food Security: The Challenges of Climate Change and Bioenergy*. Rome: FAO.
FAO (2009a) *The State of Food Insecurity in the World*. Rome: FAO.
FAO (2009b) *Global Agriculture Towards 2050*. Available at: http://www.fao.org/fileadmin/templates/wsfs/docs/Issues_papers/HLEF2050_Global_Agriculture.pdf [Accessed 30 September 2020].
FAO and IFC (International Finance Corporation) (2016) *Senegal: Irrigation Market Brief*. Report no. 26. Rome: FAO.
Faye, J. (2008) *Land and Decentralisation in Senegal*. London: IIED.
Ferdinand, M. (2022) *Decolonial Ecology: Thinking from the Caribbean World*. Cambridge: Polity Press.
Flores, P. and Guerreiro, L. (eds) (2016) *Pueblos Originarios en Lucha por las Autonomías: Experiencias y Desafíos en América Latina*. Buenos Aires: CLACSO.
Foucault, M. (2008) *The Birth of Biopolitics: Lectures at the Collège de France 1978–1979*. New York: Palgrave Macmillan.
Fraser, N. (2014) 'Behind Marx's Hidden Abode: For an Expanded Conception of Capitalism', *New Left Review*, 86(March–April), 55–72. Available at: https://newleftreview.org/issues/ii86/articles/nancy-fraser-behind-marx-s-hidden-abode [Accessed 30 October 2020].
Fulmer, A.M. (2011) 'La consulta a los pueblos indígenas y su evolución como herramienta de negociación política en América Latina. Los casos de Perú y Guatemala', *Apuntes. Revista de Ciencias Sociales*, 38(68), 37–62. doi: 10.21678/apuntes.68.619
Fumagalli, A. and Mezzadra, S. (eds) (2010) *Crisis in the Global Economy: Financial Markets, Social Struggles, and New Political Scenarios*. Los Angeles: Semiotex.
Gallais, J. (1984) *Hommes du Sahel. Espaces-Temps et Pouvoirs. Le delta intérieur du Niger. 1960–1980*. Paris: Flammarion.
Geschiere, P. (2009) *The Perils of Belonging: Autochthony, Citizenship, and Exclusion in Africa and Europe*. Chicago: University of Chicago Press.
GRAIN (2013) *Land Grabbing for Biofuels Must Stop*. Available at: https://grain.org/e/4653 [Accessed 30 September 2020].
GRAIN (2019) *The Fight Against Senhuile Goes On!* Available at: https://grain.org/e/6383 [Accessed 30 September 2020].

GSE (Gestore dei Servizi Energetici) (2008) *Incentivazione delle Fonti Rinnovabili con il Sistema dei Certificati Verdi.* GSE bulletin, 30 June. Available at: www.gse.it/dati-e-scenari/rapporti [Accessed 30 September 2020].

GSE (2009) *Incentivazione delle Fonti Rinnovabili con il Sistema dei Certificati Verdi.* GSE bulletin, 1st semester. Available at: www.gse.it/dati-e-scenari/rapporti [Accessed 30 September 2020].

GSE (2012) *Incentivazione delle fonti rinnovabili. Certificati Verdi e Tariffe Onnicomprensive.* GSE bulletin, 1st and 2nd semester. Available at: https://www.gse.it/dati-e-scenari/rapporti [Accessed 30 September 2020].

Gudynas, E. (2009) 'Diez Tesis Urgentes Sobre El Nuevo Extractivismo: Contextos y Demandas Bajo El Progresismo Sudamericano Actual', in Schuldt, J., Acosta, A., Barandiarán, A., Bebbington, A., Folchi, M. and Alayza, A. (eds) *Bolivia, Extractivismo, Política y Sociedad.* Quito: Centro Andino de Acción Popular & Centro Latinoamericano de Ecología Social, pp 187–225.

Gudynas, E. (2015) *Extractivismos: Ecología, economía y política de un modo de entender el desarrollo y la Naturaleza.* Cochabamba: Centro de Documentación e Información Bolivia/Centro Latino Americano de Ecología Social.

Gudynas, E. (2018) 'Extractivisms: Tendencies and Consequences', in Munck, R. and Delgado Wise, R. (eds) *Reframing Latin American Development.* London: Routledge, pp 61–76.

Gudynas, E., Schuldt, J., Acosta, A., Barandiarán, A., Bebbington, A., Folchi, M.A., et al (2009) *Extractivismo, política y sociedad.* Quito: CAAP-CLAES.

Haraway, D. and Tsing, A.L. (2019) 'Reflections on the Plantationocene: A Conversation with Donna Haraway & Anna Tsing', *Edge Effects.* Available at: https://edgeeffects.net/wpcontent/uploads/2019/06/PlantationoceneReflections_Haraway_Tsing.pdf [Accessed 30 September 2020].

Haraway, D., Ishikawa, N., Gilbert, S.F., Olwig, K., Tsing, A.L. and Bubandt, N. (2016) 'Anthropologists Are Talking About the Anthropocene', *Ethnos,* 81(3), 535–564. doi: 10.1080/00141844.2015.1105838

Harvey, D. (2007a) *A Brief History of Neoliberalism.* Oxford: Oxford University Press.

Harvey, D. (2007b) 'Neoliberalism as Creative Destruction', *The Annals of the American Academy of Political and Social Science,* 610(22–24), 22–44. doi: 10.1177/0002716206296780

Herreros, S. and Lima, J.D. (2011) 'Reprimarización y desindustrialización en América Latina, dos caras de la misma moneda', Presentation at the Segunda Mesa Redonda sobre Comercio y Desarrollo Sostenible, Montevideo, 7 November. ONU/CEPAL, División de Comercio Internacional e Integración. Available at: https://www.cepal.org/sites/default/files/events/files/presentacion_sebastian_herreros_y_jose_duran.pdf [Accessed 30 October 2020].

Hervouët, J.-P. (1971) *Les éleveurs riziculteurs du moyen delta du Sénégal les Peuls et l'aménagement*. Dakar: Université Cheikh Anta Diop.

Horrigan, L., Lawrence, R.S. and Walker, P. (2002) 'How Sustainable Agriculture Can Address the Environmental and Human Health Harms of Industrial Agriculture', *Environmental Health Perspectives*, 110(5), 445–456. doi:10.1289/ehp.02110445

Houston, D. (2013) 'Environmental Justice Storytelling: Angels and Isotopes at Yucca Mountain, Nevada', *Antipode*, 45(2), 417–435. doi: 10.1111/j.1467-8330.2012.01006.x

Humbert, J., Mietton, M. and Kane, A. (1995) 'L'après-barrages dans le delta du Sénégal. Scénarios de remise en eau de la cuvette du Ndiael et impacts', *Science et changements planétaires/Sécheresse*, 6(2), 207–214.

IEA (International Energy Agency) (2009) *World Energy Outlook 2009*. Paris: IEA.

Jung-A, S., Oliver, C. and Burgis, T. (2008) 'Daewoo to Cultivate Madagascar Land for Free', *Financial Times*. Available at: https://www.ft.com/content/6e894c6a-b65c-11dd-89dd-0000779fd18c [Accessed 30 October 2020].

Kettel, K. (1992) 'Gender Distortions and Development Disasters: Women and Milk in African Herding Systems', *NWSA Journal*, 4(1), 23–41. https://www.jstor.org/stable/4316174

Koopman, J. (2012) 'Will Africa's Green Revolution Squeeze African Family Farmers to Death? Lessons from Small-scale High-cost Rice Production in the Senegal River Valley', *Review of African Political Economy*, 39(133), 500–511.

Kothari, A., Salleh, A., Escobar, F., Demaria, F. and Acosta, A. (eds) (2019) *Pluriverse: A Post-Development Dictionary*. New Delhi: Tulika Books.

Kröger, M. (2021) *Extractivisms, Existences and Extinctions: Monoculture Plantations and Amazon Deforestation*. Abingdon: Routledge.

Landais, E. (1990) 'Sur les doctrines des vétérinaires coloniaux français en Afrique noire', *Cahiers des sciences humaines*, 26(1–2), 33–71. Paris: ORSTOM.

Land Matrix (2016) *Large-Scale Land Acquisitions Profile: Senegal*. Available at: https://landmatrix.org/country/senegal/ [Accessed 30 September 2020].

Lappé, F.M., Clapp, J., Anderson, M., Broad, R., Messer, E., Pogge, T., et al (2013) 'How We Count Hunger Matters', *Ethics & International Affairs*, 27(3), 251–259. doi: 10.1017/s0892679413000191

Leff, E. (2002 [1998]) *Saber ambiental: sustentabilidad, racionalidad, complejidad, poder*. Mexico/Madrid: Siglo XXI Editores.

Leff, E. (2022) 'Descolonización del conocimiento eurocéntrico, emancipación de los saberes indígenas y territorialización de la vida', *Utopía y Praxis Latinoamericana*, 27(98), e6615824. doi: 10.5281/zenodo.6615824

Leonardi, E. (2019) 'Bringing Class Analysis Back In: Assessing the Transformation of the Value-Nature Nexus to Strengthen the Connection between Degrowth and Environmental Justice', *Ecological Economics*, 156(C), 83–90. doi: 10.1016/j.ecolecon.2018.09.012

Leonardi, E. and Benegiamo, M. (2021) 'André Gorz's Labour-based Political Ecology and its Legacy for the XXI Century', in Räthzel, N., Stevis, D. and Uzzell, D. (eds) *The Palgrave Handbook of Environmental Labour Studies*. Cham: Palgrave Macmillan, pp 721–741. doi: 10.1007/978-3-030-71909-8_31

Le Roy, E. (1985) 'La loi sur le domaine national (du Sénégal) è vingt ans. Joyeux anniversaire?', *Mondes en Développement*, 13(52), 667–685.

Li, T. (2014a) *Land's End: Capitalist Relations on an Indigenous Frontier*. Durham, NC: Duke University Press.

Li, T.M. (2000) *Articulating Indigenous Identity in Indonesia: Resource Politics and the Tribal Slot*. Working paper no. 7, UC Berkeley, Institute of International Studies. Available at: https://escholarship.org/uc/item/6h82r72h [Accessed 30 October 2020].

Li, T.M. (2011) 'Centering Labor in the Land Grab Debate', *The Journal of Peasant Studies*, 38(2), 281–298. doi:10.1080/03066150.2011.559009

Li, T.M. (2014b) 'What is Land? Assembling a Resource for Global Investment', *Transactions of the Institute of British Geographers*, 39(4), 589–602. doi: 10.1111/tran.12065

Li, T.M. (2017) 'After Development: Surplus Population and the Politics of Entitlement', *Development and Change*, 48(6), 1247–1261. doi: 10.1111/dech.12333

Machart, Y.R. (2014) 'Les entreprises françaises impliquées dans l'acquisition et la gestion de grands domaines agricoles et plantations à l'international, Agronomes et vétérinaires sans frontières', *Observatoire des multinationales* (on line media). Available at: https://multinationales.org/Les-entreprises-francaises-actives [Accessed 30 October 2020].

Mamadou, L. (1996) *Africa alla Rovescia*. Rome: Prospettiva Edizioni.

Manes, L. and Franchi, G. (2012) *Land Grabbers: Italy's Involvement in the Great Land Grab*. Rome: Re:Common.

Margulis, M. (2012) 'Global Food Security Governance: The Committee on World Food Security, Comprehensive Framework for Action and the G8/G20', in Rayfus, R.G. and Weisfelt, N. (eds) *The Challenge of Food Security: International Policy and Regulatory Frameworks*. Cheltenham: Edward Elgar, pp 231–254.

Martínez-Alier, J. (2002) *The Environmentalism of the Poor: A Study of Ecological Conflicts and Valuation*. Cheltenham: Edward Elgar.

Mathieu, P., Niasse, M. and Vincke, P.P. (1989) 'Aménagements hydro-agricoles, concurrence pour l'espace et pratiques foncières locales dans la vallée du fleuve Sénégal: le cas de la zone du lac de Guiers', in Crousse, B., Le Bris, E. and Le Roy, E. (eds) *Espaces disputés en Afrique Noire: pratiques foncières locales*. Paris: Karthala, pp 217–238.

Matten, D., Crane, A. and Chapple, W. (2003) 'Behind the Mask: Revealing the True Face of Corporate Citizenship', *Journal of Business Ethics*, 45, 109–120. doi: 10.1023/A:1024128730308

Maxwell, S. (1996) 'Food Security: A Post-modern Perspective', *Food Policy*, 21(2), 155–170. doi: 10.1016/0306-9192(95)00074-7

Mbembe, A. (2003) 'Necropolitics', *Public Culture*, 15(1), 11–40. doi: 10.1215/08992363-15-1-11

McKay, B.M., Fradejas, A.A. and Ezquerro-Cañete, A. (eds) (2021) *Agrarian Extractivism in Latin America*. Oxon/New York: Routledge.

McMichael, P. (2009) 'A Food Regime Genealogy', *Journal of Peasant Studies*, 36(1), 139–169. doi: 10.1080/03066150902820354

Mezzadra, S. (2011) 'Bringing Capital Back In: A Materialist Turn in Postcolonial Studies?', *Inter-Asia Cultural Studies*, 12(1), 154–164. doi: 10.1080/14649373.2011.532987

Mezzadra, S. and Neilson, B. (2014) 'The State of Capitalist Globalization', *Viewpoint Magazine*, 4. Available at: https://viewpointmag.com/2014/09/04/the-state-of-capitalist-globalization/ [Accessed 30 September 2020].

Mietton, M. and Humbert, J. (1992) 'Pré-faisabilité hydraulique, bilan hydrologique et impacts d'une remise en eau de la cuvette du N'Diael (delta du fleuve Sénégal, Sénégal)'. Congress proceedings: 'Geography is discovery', 27th international geographical congress. Washington, DC.

Minvielle, J.P. and Lailler, A. (2005) *Les Politiques de Sécurité Alimentaire au Sénégal Depuis l'Indépendance*. Paris: L'Harmattan.

Mitchell, D. (2008) *A Note on Rising Food Prices*. Policy research working paper no. 4682, World Bank, Washington, DC. Available at: https://documents1.worldbank.org/curated/en/229961468140943023/pdf/WP4682.pdf [Accessed 30 September 2020].

Mitchell, D. (2010) *Biofuels in Africa: Opportunities, Prospects, and Challenges*. Washington, DC: World Bank.

Monénembo, T. (2004) *Peuls*. Paris: Editions du Seuil.

Monni, M. and Stirpe, F. (2010) *Valorizzazione Energetica degli Oli Vegetali Puri*. Rome: ENAMA. Available at: https://www.progettobiomasse.it/it/pdf/booklet/giallo.pdf [Accessed 30 September 2020].

Moore, J.W. (2000) 'Sugar and the Expansion of the Early Modern World-Economy: Commodity Frontiers, Ecological Transformation, and Industrialisation', *Review (Fernand Braudel Center)*, 23(3), 409–433.

Moore, J.W. (2015) *Capitalism in the Web of Life: Ecology and the Accumulation of Capital*. London/New York: Verso Books.

Moore, J. and Liley, S. (2011) 'The Socio-ecological Crises of Capitalism', in Lilley, S. (ed) *Capitalism and its Discontents: Conversations with Radical Thinkers in a Time of Tumult*. Oakland: PM Press, pp 136–152.

Moriceau, J.M. (1999) *L'élevage sous l'Ancien Régime: les fondements agraires de la France moderne, XVIe-XVIIIe siècles*. Paris: Sedes.

Morris, M., Binswanger, H., Byerlee, D., Savanti, P. and Staatz, J. (2009) *Awakening Africa's Sleeping Giant: Prospects for Commercial Agriculture in the Guinea Savannah Zone and Beyond*. Washington, DC: World Bank

Muradian, R. and Martínez-Alier, J. (2001) *Globalization and Poverty: An Ecological Perspective*. Berlin: Heinrich Böll Foundation.

Ndar Info (2015) 'Agrobusiness – Sen Huile: Le DG satisfait des performances agricoles de sa société (vidéo)', *Ndar Info*, 7 April. Available at: https://farmlandgrab.org/24752 [Accessed 30 October 2020].

Ndar Info (2017) 'Tampieri Financial Group a cédé la totalité de ses actions dans Senhuile SA (communiqué)', *Ndar Info*, 5 October. Available at: https://www.farmlandgrab.org/post/view/27535 [Accessed 30 October 2020].

Newell, P. (2012) *Globalization and the Environment: Capitalism, Ecology and Power*. Cambridge: Polity Press.

Nolte, K. Chamberlain, W. and Giger, M. (2016) International Land Deals for Agri- culture: Fresh Insights from the Land Matrix: Analytical Report II, Bern/Montpellier/Hamburg: CDE/CIRAD/GIG. Available at: https://landmatrix.org/documents/47/Analytical_Report_II_LMI_English_2016.pdf [Accessed 30 October 2020].

Nori, M., Taylor, M. and Sensi, A. (2008) *Droits pastoraux, modes de vie et adaptation au changement climatique*. London: IIED.

Oliveira, G.L.T., McKay, B.M. and Liu, J. (2021) 'Beyond Land Grabs: New Insights on Land Struggles and Global Agrarian Change', *Globalizations*, 18(3), 321–338. doi:10.1080/14747731.2020.1843842

Palmer, J.R. (2014) 'Biofuels and the Politics of Land-use Change: Tracing the Interactions of Discourse and Place in European Policy Making', *Environment and Planning A*, 46(2), 337–352.

Patel, R. (2007) *Stuffed and Starved*. London: Portobello Books.

Patel, R. (2009) 'Food Sovereignty', *The Journal of Peasant Studies*, 36(3), 663–706. doi:10.1080/03066150903143079.

Patel, R. (2013) 'The Long Green Revolution', *Journal of Peasant Studies*, 40(1), 1–63.

Patel, R. and Moore, J.W. (2017) *A History of the World in Seven Cheap Things: A Guide to Capitalism, Nature, and the Future of the Planet*. London/New York: Verso Books.

Péclard, A., Kernen, G. and Khan-Mohammad, G. (2020) 'États d'émergence. Le gouvernement de la croissance et du développement en Afrique', *Critique Internationale*, 4(89), 9–27. doi: 10.3917/crii.089.0009

Pellizzoni, L. (2015) *Ontological Politics in a Disposable World: The New Mastery of Nature*. Abingdon: Routledge.

Pigeaud, N.S. and Sylla, L. (2018) *L'Arme Invisible de la Françafrique: Une Histoire du Franc CFA*. Paris: La Découverte.

Plumwood, V. (2002 [1993]) *Feminism and the Mastery of Nature*. London/ New York: Routledge.

Quatrida, D. (2012) *Grandi progetti di sviluppo e risposte locali*. Milan: Franco Angeli.

Rondeau, A. (1975) 'La Conférence mondiale de l'Alimentation ou le triomphe de la rhétorique. Rome, 5–16 November 1974', *Revue Tiers Monde*, 16(63), 671–684. doi: 10.3406/tiers.1975.2578

SAED (Société nationale d'aménagement et d'exploitation des terres du delta du fleuve Sénégal) (1990) *La SAED a 25 ans*. Saint Louis: SAED.

SAED (2011) *Recueil des statistiques de la vallée du fleuve Sénégal*. Saint Louis: SAED.

SAED (2012) *Compte rendu de l'audience publique de l'Étude d'impact environnemental et social du projet agro-industriel de Senhuile dans la zone périphérique de la Réserve du Ndiaël, Région de Saint-Louis*. Unpublished document from the SAED Technical Services archive, consulted by the author.

Salleh, A. (2017) *Ecofeminism as Politics: Nature, Marx and the Postmodern*. London: Zed Books.

San Román, Á. and Molinero-Gerbeau, Y. (2023) 'Anthropocene, Capitalocene or Westernocene? On the Ideological Foundations of the Current Climate Crisis', *Capitalism Nature Socialism*, 34(4), 39–57. doi: 10.1080/10455752.2023.2189131

Santoir, C. (1977) *Les sociétés pastorales du Sénégal face à la sécheresse 1972–1973: réactions à la crise et degré de rétablissement deux ans après: Le cas des Peul du 'Galodjina'*. Dakar: ORSTOM.

Santoir, C. (1983) *Raison pastorale et politique de développement: les Peuls sénégalais face aux aménagements*. Paris: ORSTOM.

Sanyal, K.K. (2007) *Rethinking Capitalist Development: Primitive Accumulation, Governmentality and Post-colonial Capitalism*. Calcutta: Routledge India.

Sassen, S. (2010) 'A Savage Sorting of Winners and Losers: Contemporary Versions of Primitive Accumulation', *Globalizations*, 7(1–2), 23–50. doi: 10.1080/14747731003593091

Sassen, S. (2013) 'Land Grabs Today: Feeding the Disassembling of National Territory', *Globalizations*, 10(1), 25–46. doi:10.1080/14747731.2013.760927

Scagliarini, R. (2014) 'Ferrero, non più solo Nutella. Ora è anche il re delle nocciole', *Corriere.it*. Available at: http://www.corriere.it/economia/finanza_e_risparmio/notizie/ferrero-non-piu-solo-nutella-ora-anche-re-nocciole-f4f27b02-5a8c-11e4-a20c-1c0cce31a000.shtml [Accessed 25 January 2016].

Scherer, L.A.G. and Palazzo, G. (2011) 'The New Political Role of Business in a Globalized World: A Review of a New Perspective on CSR and Its Implications for the Firm, Governance, and Democracy', *Journal of Management Studies*, 48(4), 899–931.

Scoones, I. and Toulmin, C. (2021) 'The Sahelian Great Green Wall: Start with Local Solutions', *Pastres* (Research project/consortium blog). Available at: https://pastres.org/2021/01/29/the-sahelian-great-green-wall-start-with-local-solutions/ [Accessed 30 September 2020].

Scott, J.C. (1998) *Seeing Like a State: How Certain Schemes to Improve the Human Condition Have Failed*. New Haven: Yale University Press.

Senghor, L.S. (1971) *Nation et Voie Africaine du Socialisme* (Liberté Tome 2). Paris: Editions du Seuil.

Senhuile SA (2013) *Étude d'impact Environnemental et Social*. Dakar: Synénergie.

Sensi, R. (2012) *Il pieno, che lascia a secco i poveri*. Action Aid Italia. Available at: https://www.actionaid.it/informati/pubblicazioni/il-pieno-che-lascia-a-secco-i-poveri [Accessed 30 September 2020].

Shand, H. (2014) 'The Big Six: A Profile of Corporate Power in Seeds, Agrochemicals & Biotech', *seedsavers.org*. Available at: https://www.seedsavers.org/site/pdf/HeritageFarmCompanion_BigSix.pdf [Accessed 30 September 2020].

Shehu, D.J. and Hassan, W.A. (1995) 'Women in Dairying in the African Savanna: Their Contribution to Agro-Pastoral Household Income in the Dry Northwest of Nigeria', *Nomadic Peoples*, 36/37, 53–63.

Shiva, V. (2016) *The Violence of the Green Revolution: Third World Agriculture, Ecology, and Politics*. Lexington: University Press of Kentucky.

Smaller, H. and Mann, A. (2009) *A Thirst for Distant Lands: Foreign Investment in Agricultural Land and Water*. Winnipeg: International Institute for Sustainable Development (IISD).

Soil Association (2010) 'Telling Porkies: The Big Fat Lies About Doubling Food Production', *soilassociation.org*. Available at: https://www.soilassociation.org/LinkClick.aspx?fileticket=qbavgJQPY%2Fc%3D&tabid=390 [Accessed 30 September 2020].

Sow, A. (2001) 'Les noms sociaux en fulfulde', *Cahiers d'Études Africaines*, 163–164, 557–564.

Svampa, M.S. (2019) *Neo-Extractivism in Latin America: Socio-Environmental Conflicts, the Territorial Turn, and New Political Narratives*. Cambridge: Cambridge University Press.

Taşdemir Yaşın, Z. (2017) 'The Adventure of Capital with Nature: From the Metabolic Rift to the Value Theory of Nature', *The Journal of Peasant Studies*, 44(2), 377–401. doi: 10.1080/03066150.2016.1246435

Tienhaara, K. (2013) 'Varieties of Green Capitalism: Economy and Environment in the Wake of the Global Financial Crisis', *Environmental Politics*, 23(2), 187–204. doi: 10.1080/09644016.2013.821828

Touré, A., Ickowicz, A., Wane, I., Garba, I., Gerber, P., Atte, I., et al (2012) *Atlas des évolutions des systèmes pastoraux au Sahel*. Paris: CIRAD.

Tourrand, J.-F. (2000) *L'élevage dans la révolution agricole au Waalo, delta du fleuve Sénégal*. Montpellier: CIRAD.

Tourrand, J.-F., Jamin, J. and Landais, E. (1985) *L'élevage dans les systèmes de production du delta du fleuve Sénégal. Bilan des connaissances acquises*. Document de travail No. 6, ISRA, Dakar.

UK Government (2010) *Government Response to the Committee's Fourth Report of Session 2008–09, 'Securing Food Supplies up to 2050: The Challenges Faced by the UK'*. House of Commons. Available at: https://publications.parliament.uk/pa/cm200809/cmselect/cmenvfru/213/213i.pdf [Accessed 30 October 2020].

United Nations (1975) *Report of the World Food Conference, Rome 5–16 November 1974*. Rome: United Nations.

United Nations (2009) 'Food Production Must Double by 2050 to Meet Demand from World's Growing Population', *Meeting Coverage Department of Public Information, News and Media Division, UN Press*, New York. Available at: https://www.un.org/press/en/2009/gaef3242.doc.htm [Accessed 30 October 2020].

United Nations (2011) *Guiding Principles on Business and Human Rights*. New York/Geneva: United Nations.

United Nations Industrial Development Organization (2009) *Scaling up Bio-energy in Africa*. 12th Ordinary Session of Heads of State and Governments of the African Union, January 2009, UNIDO, Addis Ababa.

Van der Ploeg, J.D. (2012) *The New Peasantries: Struggles for Autonomy and Sustainability in an Era of Empire and Globalization*. London: Routledge.

Vanhamme, B. and Grobben, B. (2009) '"Too Good to Be True!" The Effectiveness of CSR History in Countering Negative Publicity', *Journal of Business Ethics*, 85, 273–283. doi: 10.1007/s10551-008-9731-2

Vergès, F. (2021) *A Decolonial Feminism*. London: Pluto Press.

Wagstaff, J. (2014) 'Cargill Australia Managing Director Phillipa Purser Says Foreign Investment Globally is Important', *Weekly Times Now*. Available at: http://www.weeklytimesnow.com.au/news/world/cargill-australia-managing-director-phillipa-purser-says-foreign-investment-globally-is-important/story-fnkfnuyz-1226931649073 [Accessed 30 September 2020].

Westoby, M., Walker, B. and Noy-Meir, I. (1999) 'Opportunistic Management for Rangelands Not at Equilibrium', *Journal of Range Management*, 42(4), 266–274. doi: 10.2307/3899492

Williams, J. (1988) 'Ethnology as Myth: A Century of French Writing on the Peuls of West Africa', *Journal of the History of the Behavioral Sciences*, 24, 363–377. doi: 10.1002/1520-6696(198810)24:4%3C363::AID-JHBS2300240403%3E3.0.CO;2-M

Woodhouse, P., Bernstein, H. and Hulme, D. (2000) *African Enclosures? The Social Dynamics of Wetlands in Drylands*. Oxford: James Currey.

World Bank (1982) *World Development Report: Agriculture and Development*. Washington, DC: World Bank.

World Bank (1986) *Poverty and Hunger: Issues and Options for Food Security in Developing Countries*. Washington, DC: World Bank.

World Bank (2007a) *World Development Report 2008: Agriculture for Development*. Washington, DC: World Bank.

World Bank (2007b) *World Bank Assistance to Agriculture in Sub-Saharan Africa: An IEG Review (English)*. Washington, DC: World Bank.

World Bank (2013) 'World Bank Finances Senegal's Agribusiness Plans to Boost its Food Production and Jobs; Will Also Help the Wider Sahel Region', *The World Bank Press Release*, 12 December. Available at: https://www.worldbank.org/en/news/press-release/2013/12/19/world-bank-senegal-agribusiness-sahel [Accessed 30 September 2020].

World Bank (2019) *Sénégal: Notes de Politiques Économiques et Sociales*. Washington, DC: World Bank.

Ye, J., van der Ploeg, J.D., Schneider, S. and Shanin, T. (2020) 'The Incursions of Extractivism: Moving from Dispersed Places to Global Capitalism', *The Journal of Peasant Studies*, 47(1), 155–183. doi: 10.1080/03066150.2018.1559834

Zibechi, R. (2020) 'El estado de excepción como paradigma político del extractivismo', in Ortega Santos, A. and Olivieri, C. (eds) *Saberes bioculturales en pie de re-existencias en el sur global*. Granada: Editorial Universidad de Granada, pp 133–149.

Zibechi, R. and Machado, D. (2023) *Estados para el despojo: Del Estado benefactor al Estado neoliberal extractivista*. La Paz: Plural Editors.

Index

References to figures appear in *italic* type. References to endnotes show both the page number and the note number (106n5).